The Black Architect

THE BLACK PROTOCOL OF WEALTH

Unlock the Forbidden Codes to Purge
Money Blocks, Elevate Your Frequency,
and Build Lasting Wealth

Staten House

This book was written in quiet extraction, ruthless clarity, and sovereign design by one who chose structure over struggle, command over chaos, and wealth over obedience. May it serve the version of you ready to exit and reign.

Table of Contents

Table of Contents

PART III ....
....
....
....
....

6

Introduction — The Hidden Game of Wealth

Why Manifestation Alone Isn't Enough

You've journaled. You've visualized. You've meditated with crystals, spoken affirmations in the mirror, and written checks to yourself with million-dollar amounts. Still — the bank account says otherwise.

Let's tell the truth:
Manifestation isn't broken. It's incomplete.

Most of what you've been taught about attracting wealth is a fragment. A sliver of the truth, polished and sold as the whole system. You were told to *think positive*, *vibrate higher*, and *believe it's already yours* — but rarely were you shown the real mechanics underneath it all.

Because the truth is this:

Manifestation without recalibration is mental cosplay.

If your subconscious is still running scripts of unworthiness…
If your environment is leaking energy faster than you can visualize it back in…
If your systems don't match your soul's demands…
Then no amount of "good vibes" will create sustainable wealth.

This isn't your fault.
You were initiated into a broken system. Trained to hustle or hope — with no middle code. What you needed was initiation, not just information. What you needed was a protocol.

That's what this book is.

The Black Protocol of Wealth isn't a new manifestation trick. It's the decoding of what actually builds unshakable wealth — inside and out. It's not a feel-good fantasy. It's a precision system that works because it purges what doesn't.

Here, we don't "try to manifest."
We **command**, **calibrate**, and **construct** wealth on every level: mental, emotional, energetic, and structural.

If you're ready to stop playing the surface game and start shifting your entire field of reality — welcome to the hidden game. You're about to learn why manifestation alone keeps people stuck...

...and what actually sets you free.

Why Hard Work Keeps Most People Trapped

You've been taught since childhood that hard work is the holy grail. That struggle equals worth. That the more you grind, the more you deserve.

But let's look closer.

If hard work was the key, the janitor would be a millionaire.
If effort alone built empires, your most exhausted friend would be the most successful.
They're not. You're not. Not yet. And deep down, you know why.

Hard work is not the answer. It's the distraction.

It keeps you so busy *doing* that you forget to *align*.
It keeps you chasing dollars instead of designing flows.
It keeps your nervous system in survival mode, which energetically repels the very wealth you're trying to earn.

This is how the system was rigged:
Train the masses to equate suffering with success — so they never question the blueprint.
Reward burnout. Celebrate exhaustion. Glorify the grind.

But here's the secret the wealthy know — even if they don't say it out loud:
They don't hustle harder. They calibrate higher.

Real wealth isn't created by stacking more hours.
It's created by aligning your energy, your decisions, and your systems to produce **clean, leveraged output** — with minimal energetic cost.

That doesn't mean you won't do the work. It means your *work will work*.
You'll stop spinning, draining, and hoping. You'll start building flow-based architecture for your life.

This is not about laziness.
It's about *energetic precision* — choosing power over pressure.

This book is your release from the trap.
Not because you'll do less, but because you'll do it from alignment, not addiction.

What the "Black Protocol" Is — And Why You've Never Seen It

The word "black" has been distorted.

In many spiritual traditions, black is sacred. It is the color of mystery, depth, hidden power. The void that births galaxies. The soil that nourishes roots. The silence where wisdom speaks.

But in modern programming, black is associated with fear, danger, the unknown. So when you hear "Black Protocol," something stirs — curiosity, resistance, a whisper of rebellion.

That's intentional.

The Black Protocol is not evil. It's encrypted.

This book is not about following another guru, memorizing affirmations, or plugging into someone else's formula. This is about **unlocking the codes that were hidden in your own energetic DNA** — the ones no one ever taught you how to read.

Why haven't you seen this before?

Because you were trained to outsource your power.
To chase money through approved methods.
To treat wealth like a prize, not a consequence of alignment.

The real reason you haven't activated lasting wealth is not because you're lazy, unlucky, or not "high vibe" enough.

It's because you were **never given the full protocol.**

- You were told to visualize, but not how to purge the mental parasites that rewrite your efforts while you sleep.

- You were told to budget, but not how to track the energetic leaks that drain every dollar you earn.

- You were told to hustle, but not how to build aligned systems that make your aura magnetic and your income scalable.

The Black Protocol gives you that.
It fuses the unseen laws with visible results.
It connects soul and system.
It replaces wishful thinking with ritual.
It replaces burnout with precision.

This is not a surface fix. It's a structural shift.
Not just manifestation — **activation**.

You won't just read this book.
You'll move through it. Command it. Let it initiate you.

The parts of you that were hidden — that knew you were meant for more — will finally have a structure to rise through.

Who This Book Is For: Escapers, Builders, and Risers

Not everyone is ready for this work.

This book is not for those looking for quick hacks, surface motivation, or spiritual entertainment. It's for those who feel the pull — deep in the gut, beneath the noise — that there is another way to live, earn, and create.

There are three kinds of people this book was written for.
If you find yourself in one, or moving between them, you're exactly where you need to be.

1. The Escaper

You're in the job, the life, or the pattern you know is draining you — but you haven't yet found the exit. You can feel your energy slipping, your mind cluttered, your soul whispering *"this isn't it."*

You're not lazy. You're not broken.
You've just been trained to survive, not to align.
The Escaper doesn't need a plan yet — they need a **purge**.
A detox from the noise, the programming, the hustle mythology.
That's where your power begins.

2. The Builder

You've already stepped out. Maybe you've started something — a business, a brand, a mission. But you're in the fog. Working hard, pushing forward, but it's not clicking the way it should. The money is inconsistent. The energy is unstable.

The Builder doesn't need more effort.
They need **precision**, clarity, flow systems, and identity anchoring.
They need to stop bleeding energy through false strategies and start **magnetizing results through calibration**.

3. The Riser

You're already doing well — maybe even admired for it. But something's missing. You know there's a deeper level. More ease. More flow. More

11

truth. You're tired of playing a role. You want real freedom — not just income, but sovereignty.

The Riser doesn't need more success.
They need **integration.**
They need to unify the spiritual and structural parts of them that have been operating in silos.

Whether you're escaping, building, or rising — this book meets you where you are and then breaks the ceiling on what you think is possible.

Because the moment you align your energy, thoughts, and systems, **wealth becomes inevitable** — not through effort, but through embodiment.

How to Use This Book: Protocols, Rituals, and Activations

This isn't a book you skim.
It's a protocol you **enter.**

Each chapter is a **code.**
Each ritual is an **initiation.**
Each activation is a **frequency shift waiting to be chosen.**

You won't find fluff here. No endless theories, no recycled motivational fluff. Every page is built to shift your field, not just your mindset.

Here's how to move through it:

- **Start at the beginning.**
  The protocols are layered in a specific sequence. You're not just learning — you're being recalibrated, step by step, to handle more wealth with less resistance.

- **Don't skip the rituals.**
  They're not extras. They're energetic keys. Whether it's a 3-day purge, a 72-hour challenge, or a journaling prompt — these rituals are your actual entry points to a new frequency.

- **Choose presence over speed.**
  This is not a race. It's a decoding. You'll get the most power by treating this like a sacred manual — not a weekend read. Pause where needed. Reread. Reflect. Execute.

- **Apply it across your path.**
  Whether you're an employee, freelancer, healer, artist, coach, consultant, or all of the above — these protocols flex to fit your life. You'll see examples and tools for multiple work paths, so you can tailor the wealth codes to your world.

- **Let your body guide you.**
  You'll feel certain parts hit harder than others. That's your nervous system pointing you toward a block — or a breakthrough. Follow the pull. That's where your upgrade lives.

- **Use the Appendix.**
  At the end of the book, you'll find tools, templates, rituals, and shortcut sheets. These are not afterthoughts — they're your integration anchors. Use them as needed to stay aligned as you scale.

This is not self-help. This is system override.
Not law of attraction — law of alignment.
Not dream journaling — wealth architecture.

By the end of this book, you will have purged the parasites, rewired your code, activated your aura, and built a flow that attracts wealth with precision.

If you're ready, turn the page.

The Protocol begins now.

How to Use This Book: Protocols, Rituals, and Activations

This isn't a book you skim.
It's a protocol you **enter**.

Each chapter is a **code**.
Each ritual is an **initiation**.
Each activation is a **frequency shift waiting to be chosen.**

You won't find fluff here. No endless theories, no recycled motivational fluff. Every page is built to shift your field, not just your mindset.

Here's how to move through it:

- **Start at the beginning.**
  The protocols are layered in a specific sequence. You're not just learning — you're being recalibrated, step by step, to handle more wealth with less resistance.

- **Don't skip the rituals.**
  They're not extras. They're energetic keys. Whether it's a 3-day purge, a 72-hour challenge, or a journaling prompt — these rituals are your actual entry points to a new frequency.

- **Choose presence over speed.**
  This is not a race. It's a decoding. You'll get the most power by treating this like a sacred manual — not a weekend read. Pause where needed. Reread. Reflect. Execute.

- **Apply it across your path.**
  Whether you're an employee, freelancer, healer, artist, coach, consultant, or all of the above — these protocols flex to fit your life. You'll see examples and tools for multiple work paths, so you can tailor the wealth codes to your world.

- **Let your body guide you.**
  You'll feel certain parts hit harder than others. That's your nervous system pointing you toward a block — or a breakthrough. Follow the pull. That's where your upgrade lives.

This is not self-help. This is system override.

Not law of attraction — law of alignment.

Not dream journaling — wealth architecture.

By the end of this book, you will have purged the parasites, rewired your code, activated your aura, and built a flow that attracts wealth with precision.

If you're ready, turn the page.

The Protocol begins now.

PART I — The Inner Protocols: Purge, Recode, Realign

Before wealth flows into your life, it must flow through you.

Most people never build lasting wealth because they skip this part. They try to jump into tactics, strategy, or income streams while still carrying the energetic debris of old beliefs, emotional parasites, and mental noise.

You cannot build sovereignty on a corrupted foundation.

That's why **Part I** is the purge.
It is the energetic clearing. The mental rewiring. The frequency shift that makes all other protocols stick.

Think of it like opening sacred space — not just to read, but to receive.

In this section, you will:

- **Identify and extract the invisible parasites** blocking your flow

- **Recode your frequency** so your aura becomes a signal for wealth

- **Align with the hidden laws** that determine flow, opportunity, and expansion

No branding, no budgets, no digital accounts yet.
Just pure inner recalibration — the part most skip, and the reason they stay stuck.

If you move through this part fully, you'll notice it quickly:
More clarity. More pull. Less force. Better decisions. Clean yes's.
Confident no's.

This is where the real shift begins.

Now — purge what you've been carrying.
Let's begin Protocol I.

Protocol I — The Parasite Purge

The Invisible Programs That Block Wealth

You don't just have thoughts.
You have **programs** — hidden scripts operating below your awareness, shaping your decisions, your emotions, and your financial outcomes in real time.

And many of them are **parasitic**.

They didn't originate from your truth.
They were implanted — through repetition, trauma, silence, and shame.

These programs don't show up as monsters.
They show up as *reasonableness*:

- "Maybe I should wait a bit longer…"

- "I don't want to be greedy."

- "This offer probably isn't worth that price."

They don't scream. They whisper.
And the most dangerous ones?
You've been calling them *your personality*.

Where They Begin

Parasites are inherited long before you realize you're participating in them.

- A parent shaming you for asking for too much.

- Watching money destroy relationships and thinking, *better to stay small.*

- Being praised for self-sacrifice and punished for boldness.

- Seeing rich people mocked, judged, or feared.

- Growing up in systems that reward survival, not sovereignty.

Every one of these moments is a seed.
And when it's reinforced over time, it grows into an unconscious rule:
Play safe. Stay small. Don't ask. Don't want too much. Don't be too much.

These are not just limiting beliefs.

They're energetic parasites — intelligent patterns that live off your power.

And if you don't purge them, they run your financial life.
Most money blocks are not logical.

Let's name a few that live inside millions:

- "I have to work twice as hard to earn enough."

- "Rich people are greedy or corrupt."

- "If I make too much, I'll lose it anyway."

- "If I shine too bright, people will leave."

- "I'm not good with money."

- "Money always causes problems."

These aren't opinions.
They are **energetic malware**.

Each one creates a loop of behavior that *proves itself right* — no matter how much you journal, visualize, or hope.

Every time you undercharge, delay action, overspend, or avoid visibility, it's not random.
It's a **parasite pattern** firing in your nervous system.

The Emotional Cost

What's worse than struggling to earn?
Struggling while secretly knowing you're capable of so much more.

Parasites don't just block money.
They distort your sense of identity.
They convince you that overgiving is noble, that undercharging is humble, that ambition is dangerous.

You start to fear your own power.
Not because it's dangerous — but because someone convinced you it was.

You don't just avoid money.
You avoid **visibility**, **impact**, and **truth** — because all of it threatens the parasite's grip.

Here's the Real Danger

These programs don't just block wealth.
They **adapt**.

They learn your language — spiritual, rational, strategic — and **cloak themselves in it**.

So the thought *"I'm just not aligned right now"* may actually be a parasite that's scared of visibility.
The feeling *"I need more healing first"* might be a dressed-up scarcity loop.

Parasites speak in delay, doubt, and drain.
They are masters of self-sabotage in disguise.

Why You Can't Think Your Way Out

You've tried to shift. You've read the books, said the affirmations, visualized the success.

But if the parasite is still in your field, all you're doing is **pouring clean water into a poisoned cup.**

That's why mindset isn't enough.
You don't need more positivity.
You need a **purge**.

This first protocol isn't about information.
It's your **extraction sequence** — your initiation into clarity.

Once you see the parasite, it loses its power.
Once you expose the pattern, you break the spell.

Mental Parasites: What They Are and How They Spread

Not all parasites live in the body.
Some live in your **mindstream** — feeding on your focus, distorting your self-worth, and hijacking your decisions without detection.

We call these **mental parasites**.

They are not just "bad thoughts."
They are **loops of belief** so deeply embedded that you no longer question them.
They mimic your voice, rewrite your impulses, and resist change like a survival instinct — because that's exactly what they've become.

What Exactly Is a Mental Parasite?

A mental parasite is a **subconscious script** that:

- Overrides your intuition

- Disguises itself as logic or emotional safety

- Repeats patterns that block expansion

- Gains strength through repetition and silence

It isn't just a belief. It's a system.
One that rewires your nervous system to stay within a narrow band of what feels "safe," even if that safety equals stagnation.

Mental parasites shrink your permission field.

They teach you that settling is wisdom, dimming is strategy, and shrinking is spiritual.

They are subtle, but lethal.
Because they don't attack — they embed.
They live in the gaps between your thoughts. They speak the language of fear dressed as practicality.

How They Spread

Like any parasite, these patterns **spread through exposure** and **frequency**.

Here are the primary carriers:

- **Family Conditioning**
  "We don't talk about money."
  "We work hard, we don't complain."
  "That's just how it is."
  Most mental parasites are handed down with love — which makes them even harder to question.

- **Collective Programming**
  Every time you hear "money doesn't grow on trees" or "it takes 10 years to be successful," you're being exposed to energetic mold. Society doesn't teach wealth. It teaches containment.

- **Spiritual Bypass Culture**
  Ironically, the spiritual world can be a breeding ground for parasites.
  "If it's meant to be, it'll happen."
  "You just need to be more high-vibe."
  These sound light, but often mask fear of action, fear of visibility, and fear of responsibility.

- **Micro-Traumas & Repetitions**
  One rejection. One public failure. One moment of embarrassment.
  When your system doesn't have the tools to process it, a parasite moves in. And then it looks for repetition — similar moments to strengthen its claim.

- **Digital Echo Chambers**
  The internet rewards polarity. If you've been surrounded by scarcity talk, trauma loops, or cynical content, you're absorbing more than opinions — you're breathing in ambient programming.

What It Looks Like in Action

Mental parasites don't just whisper doubts.
They **shape identity**.

You start thinking things like:

- "I'm just not a money person."

- "I'm more of a behind-the-scenes type."

- "I'm not meant to charge that much."

- "Visibility isn't my style."

- "I need another certification first."

None of these are truths.
They are **installations** — running beneath the surface, locking you into a smaller self.

And here's the twist:

The more conscious you become, the *smarter* your parasites get.
They evolve. They start using your spiritual language, your intellectual awareness, even your empathy against you.

This is why clearing your mind isn't enough.
You must **reclaim your authority over it.**

Ritual: The 7-Day Parasite Purge

"You don't heal a parasite. You purge it — with silence, command, and truth."

This is not just mindset work. It's **field detox.**
A full interruption to the unconscious programs that keep your wealth small, your power dimmed, and your nervous system on survival loop.

For 7 consecutive days, you'll walk the same 3-phase ritual — not for variety, but for **deep anchoring**. This is how you shift from recognition into transformation.

PHASE 1 — Exposure

Objective: Reveal the hidden parasites and bring them into conscious view.

Day One: The Core Reveal

- **Silence Your External Feeds**
  → No social media, podcasts, or spiritual noise. Just stillness and self-signal.

- **Create Your Parasite Pattern List**
  Journal your answers to:

    1. What money or success patterns do I repeat that drain me?

    2. What thoughts show up when I try to expand or charge more?

    3. Whose voice do those thoughts sound like?

- **Audit Your Inputs**
  List your top digital/energetic influences. Label them: *Nourishing / Neutral / Draining.*
  → Eliminate at least one "Draining" source for the next 7 days.

25

Days 2–7: Ongoing Exposure

→ *Revisit your Parasite Pattern List each day.*

→ Add any new thoughts, impulses, or behaviors that rise to the surface.

Parasites hide under pressure — as you shift, more will surface.

PHASE 2 — Extraction

Objective: Disrupt the parasite's control and reclaim energetic authority.

Daily Practice:

- **Interruption Command**
  When a parasite thought or emotion arises, speak aloud:

"That's not me. That's a program. I do not consent."

- **Embodiment Anchor**
  As you say it:
  → Stand taller
  → Open your chest
  → Unclench your jaw
  → This tells your nervous system: *we're no longer obeying distortion.*

- **Light Reset Ritual**
  Midday: Step into sunlight or natural light, eyes closed.
  Visualize gray smoke leaving your field. Say:

"I return my field to original power. Nothing unchosen remains."

PHASE 3 — Replacement

Objective: Install a new energetic command system.

Daily Practice:

- **Recode Your Truth**
  Repeat and refine your three activation lines:

26

1. "I no longer accept _____."

2. "My new truth is _____."

3. "Every action I take now affirms _____."

- **Create and Use Your Command Loop**
  → Record yourself reading your three lines aloud.
  → Add any affirmations or clarifying declarations.
  → Listen 3x per day — morning, midday, evening.

- **Close the Portal**
  Final daily visualization: Seal your energetic field in light.
  Whisper:

"It ends with me. I carry only what aligns. I walk forward clean."

Daily Integration Tracker

At the end of each day, journal:

1. What parasite pattern showed up today?

2. How did I interrupt or shift it?

3. What truth am I beginning to believe instead?

Optional Expansion: The 30-Day Cleanse

A week is a powerful act of courage — and a bold affirmation of independence. But sometimes, a week is not enough.

Some parasites are deeply rooted. Some behaviors are ancient. And some transformations require a **shockwave** — a period long enough to reset your identity, rewire your nervous system, and **birth a new pattern entirely**.

If you feel the deeper pull, repeat this ritual daily for 30 days straight. Track your resistance. Eliminate new draining sources as they appear. Keep raising your standard.

Rebuild your life from alignment, not adaptation.

This is more than a reset.
It's a return — to your original field of power.

The goal of this deeper purge is simple:
To take back full control of your life.
Of what you think. Of how you act. Of what shapes your outcomes.

Because without this, nothing else works.
You cannot scale chaos.
You cannot visualize over sabotage.
You cannot magnetize wealth while running on borrowed beliefs.

This is more than a reset.
It's a return — to your original field of power.

Protocol II — Recode Your Frequency

Your Aura, Your Results: How Energy Shapes Perception

Money doesn't just follow effort.
It follows **energy** — and energy has a signal. That signal is your **aura**.

Most people treat the aura like some mystical fog — a nice visual on a meditation reel, something to "raise" with affirmations or incense. But your aura isn't abstract. It's a **living broadcast system**, constantly transmitting your internal state to the external world.

Your aura is your business card. Your signal. Your strategy.

What you radiate is what gets read.
And what gets read determines how people respond to you — whether they trust you, pay you, remember you, follow you, or avoid you.

This is not energetic poetry. It's human physics.

Let's break it down:

- You've walked into rooms where someone felt magnetic before they spoke.

- You've met someone who looked "successful," but felt off.

- You've felt invisible even when you showed up prepared.

That wasn't charisma. That was **aura calibration**.

You are constantly shaping your field — with your breath, your thoughts, your posture, your food, your environment, and your internal stories. The only question is whether you're doing it **consciously** or by default.

What Happens When Your Frequency is Off?

You might…

- Speak clearly, but get ignored

- Build offers, but attract no buyers

- Apply for jobs, but get ghosted

- Network, but stay unseen

- Create content, but get no engagement

- Say "yes," but feel resentment after

These aren't random results. They're the outcome of **energetic misalignment**.
You're broadcasting from one signal while trying to manifest from another.

You don't just need confidence. You need **field coherence** — where your body, words, presence, and value all speak the same frequency.

Because people don't respond to what you say.
They respond to what you carry.

Energetic Leaks vs. Coherence

When your aura is scattered, so is your income.
When your energy is clean and consistent, so are your results.

Leaks happen when:

- You're saying yes from fear

- You're undercharging and overgiving

- You're surrounded by environments that drain you

- You're still questioning your worth in the middle of action

30

Coherence happens when:

- You hold a clear standard, even when it's uncomfortable

- You rest and act from intention, not reaction

- You treat your aura like architecture, not fog

- You release the need to explain and start embodying your truth

You don't chase alignment. You build it.

And once your aura is aligned with truth — not trauma, not programming — perception shifts.
You become visible. Safe. Respected. Magnetic.

Pineal Clarity, Mental Focus, and Presence as Wealth Levers

You can't magnetize wealth through a fogged lens.
If your mind is cluttered, distracted, and reactionary, your frequency will be too.

This is why we don't just "get clear" — we **become clarity**.

Your pineal gland, your mental focus, and your presence form the energetic throne you broadcast from.
If your throne is unstable, your command won't land.

The Pineal Gland — Your Inner Tuner

Often called the "third eye," your pineal gland is far more than spiritual symbolism. It's your **internal antenna**, constantly tuning your perception, circadian rhythm, and intuitive signal.

But in most people, it's calcified — physically by processed foods, overstimulation, artificial light... and energetically by fear, distraction, and noise.

A fogged pineal = a distorted receiver.

And most people are **deep in distortion**:

- Overstimulated by screens and blue light

- Living under artificial lighting cycles

- Flooded with noise, opinions, and synthetic food

- Consuming more than they integrate

- Reacting faster than they reflect

You can't hear your intuition when the signal is jammed.
You can't feel timing when your inner clock is hijacked.

A blocked pineal makes you question the right move and trust the wrong one.
It keeps you second-guessing instead of sensing.

When the pineal is clear:

- You sense opportunity

- You speak with conviction

- You make bold decisions without panic

- You attract synchronicity because your internal clock is aligned

A clear pineal gland doesn't just help you "see" — it helps you _receive_.

This isn't mystical. It's functional.
To receive wealth consistently, you must become a stable signal — and that begins with **what you put into your body, your mind, and your field.**

Mental Focus — Your Frequency Filter

Focus isn't about attention span.
It's about **permission**: what thoughts, inputs, and priorities you allow to enter your field.

If your focus is fractured, your results will be too.
If your focus is disciplined, even in chaos, you become magnetic.

Wealth responds to:

- Clear messaging

- Clean offers

- Strategic visibility

- Confident decisions
  None of that is possible in a distracted state.

You've been trained to multitask — but multitasking is fragmentation. And fragmentation leads to energetic noise, decision fatigue, and broken manifestations.

Focus is not just a productivity tool.
It is a **spiritual boundary**.

When you train your mind to stay on one signal:

- You build potency behind your words

- You finish what you start

- You broadcast clarity — and clarity attracts decision

Your aura is strongest when your focus is singular.
People don't trust scattered energy. Money doesn't either.

And the truth is this:
You're not tired because you're doing too much.
You're tired because you're **leaking energy into tabs, to-do lists, notifications, and false urgency.**

Distraction is a parasite dressed as productivity.

Real power comes when your focus becomes a sword — not a sponge.

Presence — Your Amplifier

There is no magnetism without presence.

When you are fully in your body, fully with your breath, fully connected to the moment — people lean in. Opportunities lock in. Clients trust you. Decisions clarify.

Presence is the part most people ignore — because it requires stillness. And stillness feels dangerous to a nervous system addicted to proving.

34

But your most magnetic moments — in business, conversation, intimacy, sales, performance — didn't happen because you were rehearsed.

They happened because you were **present.**

Presence is what makes your energy walk into a room before your body does.
It's what makes someone lean in, trust you, remember you — even if they can't explain why.

Presence multiplies every other effort.
It makes one sentence land like a strategy deck.
One gesture feel like leadership.
One silence speak louder than shouting.

You don't need to say more.
You need to be *more felt.*

And that comes from breath. Stillness. Embodiment.
From becoming the calm in the room, not the reaction.

When your pineal is clear, your focus is clean, and your presence is stable — your aura becomes **undeniable**.

Practice: Frequency Reset System

"To command wealth, you must first command your field."

This is not a checklist.
It's a system — a set of frequency levers you can activate daily to tune your energy, clarify your signal, and become the version of you that wealth naturally responds to.

Each component of this system recalibrates a different layer of your energetic field:

- **Mind** → Signal clarity

- **Food** → Cellular alignment

- **Breath** → Nervous system regulation

- **Light** → Circadian and spiritual tuning

When used together — even in simple form — they become your **energetic architecture**.

MIND: The Aura Command Ritual

Your words are not just thoughts — they are software instructions for your aura.

What you say silently is what your field obeys.
And most people are speaking **fear commands** on autopilot:

- "I hope this works."

- "Let me see if they say yes."

- "What if they think I'm too much?"

Every one of these thoughts weakens your magnetic field. They broadcast doubt, not clarity. Subtle, but powerful.

The Ritual:

Every morning (or before any money-related action), speak your Aura Commands aloud:

1. "I move with authority."

2. "My signal is clear. My worth is not negotiable."

3. "I hold the space I used to shrink inside."

4. "I do not borrow fear. I generate alignment."

Speak them standing. Tall. Shoulders open. Eyes steady.
Let your nervous system feel the shift.

Want to amplify? Write a custom Aura Line each week based on a fear you're dissolving. Speak the antidote.

FOOD: Energetic Nourishment Ritual

Food is not just fuel — it's frequency coding.

What you eat either sharpens your intuition or fogs it.
Either supports your clarity or feeds your confusion. Your cells are not separate from your spirit. If your biology is sluggish, your decisions will be too.

This is not about perfection. It's about **presence and purity**.

The Ritual:

For 7 days (or longer), commit to *Energetic Mornings*:

- No processed sugar, refined oils, or stimulants before noon

- Begin with:

    o   Warm lemon water or herbal tea

    o   Fresh fruit or a grounding smoothie

o   Full presence — no phone, no scrolling

Before eating, pause. Close your eyes. Say:

"This nourishes my clarity. I eat to carry clean energy."

Why this works: food affects your pineal, gut-brain axis, and hormonal flow — all of which impact timing, confidence, and intuitive decision-making.

➷ BREATH: Nervous System Reset Protocol

Your breath is your real-time frequency regulator.

When your breath is shallow, your field is chaotic.
When your breath is deliberate, your field becomes unshakable.
Breath is the **only tool** that changes your physical, emotional, and energetic state in under 60 seconds.

Most people are trying to "stay calm" while breathing like prey.

The Ritual:

Use this **Command Breath Pattern** whenever fog, fear, or fatigue strikes:

The 4-7-8 Pattern

- Inhale: 4 seconds

- Hold: 7 seconds

- Exhale (slow): 8 seconds
  → Repeat for 3–5 minutes.

Do this:

- Before a sales call

- When making a bold decision

- When fear tries to override your clarity

As you breathe, say internally:

"I breathe as a builder. I act from calm. I release the static."

LIGHT: Signal Calibration Ritual

Your body — and your aura — are tuned by light.

Every single cell has a clock. That clock is tuned by the **sun**, not your schedule. When your light exposure is off, your pineal fogs, your mood dips, your decisions dull, and your sense of timing collapses.

Artificial light creates artificial chaos.
And when your pineal gland is suppressed, so is your clarity.

Your pineal gland is your inner tuner. Light is its charger.

This isn't just a spiritual concept — it's biological.
Without clean, natural light, your intuitive channel shuts down. Your aura becomes muddy. Your timing — in offers, decisions, and actions — loses accuracy.

The Ritual:

Morning Light Reset

- Within 20 minutes of waking, get 5–10 minutes of natural light exposure

- Stand by a window or outdoors. Close your eyes. Let the light hit your face, forehead, and eyelids.

As you absorb the light, speak (silently or aloud):

"I restore my intuitive clarity. My pineal is clear. My signal is clean."
"I reset to original power. No distortion remains in my field."

Why this works: light activates your pineal gland, sharpens your energetic perception, and anchors your frequency. You don't just become more alert — you become more accurate.

How to Use the Frequency Reset System

Use one ritual per day — or stack them in the morning for full recalibration.

Most powerful times:

- **Before visibility** (content, calls, conversations)

- **When triggered or unclear**

- **When transitioning from chaos to clarity**

Final Reminder

You don't have to force wealth.
You have to **clear the interference** so your original power — the one that attracts, commands, and builds — can rise.

These are not habits. These are frequency weapons.
Use them as rituals. Carry them as your new baseline.
And watch the world respond to what you now broadcast.

Protocol III — The Laws of Hidden Abundance

Why Alignment Creates More Wealth Than Hustle

You've been programmed to believe that wealth is earned through exhaustion.
Through effort. Through proving.

Work harder. Wake earlier. Grind longer. Outperform the competition.
The faster you run, the more you deserve.

But this equation is a trap.
Because most people are not failing from lack of work — they're failing from misalignment.

You don't have an effort problem.
You have an **energetic conflict** between your desires and your design.

The Great Lie of Hustle

Hustle creates two hidden forms of scarcity:

1. Energetic Burnout
You drain your nervous system, immune system, and creativity by constantly forcing forward momentum.
The more you push, the more you narrow your vision, missing unseen pathways that alignment would have revealed.

2. Frequency Distortion
When your aura is broadcasting strain, lack, and desperation, you unconsciously repel the very opportunities you're chasing.
People feel it: the forced sales call, the anxious negotiation, the overselling pitch — all rooted in hustle energy.

You may get short-term wins through hustle. But you sacrifice long-term wealth through incoherence.

Wealth does not respond to exhaustion.
It responds to **clarity, capacity, and coherence**.

The Law of Energetic Alignment

Alignment means this:

Your actions match your essence.

When your offers, pricing, visibility, and audience fit your true energetic design:

- Sales feel like service, not begging

- Marketing becomes magnetic, not manipulative

- Boundaries feel natural, not defensive

- Scaling becomes sustainable, not sacrificial

You stop draining your energy forcing outcomes.
You begin **amplifying your aura** by embodying your truth.

Alignment creates spaciousness.
Spaciousness creates presence.
Presence multiplies impact.

The Wealth Formula Most Ignore

Here is the actual formula for sustainable wealth:

Aligned Identity → Clear Signal → Consistent Actions → Scalable Results

Hustle skips the first two steps entirely.
It tries to shortcut the field by stacking effort on top of distortion. And eventually, it collapses — through burnout, breakdown, or breakdown of integrity.

42

You cannot outrun your own field. You can only clean it.

When you align, you unlock exponential wealth because:

- People trust your energy

- Clients feel your confidence

- Offers flow out of your lived expertise

- Pricing reflects your sovereignty

- Income becomes the byproduct of coherence, not compensation for pain

---

You're not here to work harder.
You're here to **hold a field so clean that wealth enters by law, not force.**

This is the first law of hidden abundance:
Alignment outpaces hustle. Precision outpowers pressure.

The 7 Invisible Laws the Wealthy Follow — Whether They Know It or Not

Wealth is not random.
It follows laws — not the surface laws you were taught, but hidden energetic patterns that most people have never been shown.

The wealthy don't always consciously understand these laws.
Some inherited them. Some stumbled into them.
But whether conscious or not, these laws govern how they attract, hold, and multiply wealth.

Now, you will see what most remain blind to.

---

1. The Law of Energetic Safety

Money flows toward what feels safe to carry it.

- Wealth does not move toward desperation or self-doubt.

- Your aura must signal *I am safe with expansion.*

- When your nervous system associates growth with threat, you repel wealth subconsciously.

The wealthy embody safety — emotionally, financially, and energetically — even before the external proof arrives.

---

2. The Law of Identity Containment

Your income rises to meet your internal identity thermostat.

- You do not rise to your goals — you rise to your identity.

- The wealthy unconsciously hold an identity that expects wealth as normal, not exceptional.

- The poor see abundance as "more than enough."

- The wealthy see it as *just how it works.*

Until your identity expects wealth, no strategy will stick.

---

3. The Law of Value Compression

The wealthy compress more value into less effort.

- They don't exchange hours for dollars endlessly.
- They create structures where small actions produce extended returns — products, investments, systems, intellectual property.
- Their field is leveraged.
- Their value is condensed, not scattered.

They don't work harder. They build structures that work without them.

---

4. The Law of Decision Velocity

The wealthy decide faster because their field is clearer.

- They don't need external validation for every move.
- Clarity reduces hesitation.
- Their intuition has been trained through repetition, failure, and recalibration.

Speed is not recklessness — it's alignment in motion.

---

5. The Law of Energetic Neutrality

The wealthy separate emotion from expansion.

- Scarcity creates emotional attachment to every transaction.

45

- The wealthy operate from neutrality — not coldness, but stability.

- Win or lose, sale or no sale, they remain centered.

- This neutrality allows for clearer negotiation, higher pricing, and less energetic bleed.

Emotional detachment is a multiplier. Desperation is a repellent.

---

6. The Law of Controlled Visibility

The wealthy control how and when they're seen.

- They understand that visibility is not about exposure — it's about signal control.

- They show up where they can create maximum resonance, not random attention.

- They leverage presence, positioning, and timing to amplify their aura.

Visibility without calibration invites energetic chaos.
Calibrated visibility creates magnetic authority.

---

7. The Law of Calibration Over Compensation

When something feels off, they calibrate — they don't compensate.

- Most people try to fix problems by *doing more*.

- The wealthy adjust the field: energy leaks, offer structure, pricing, audience, partnerships, mindset.

- They don't hustle their way out of misalignment — they adjust frequency first.

Hustle stacks pressure. Calibration dissolves friction.

The Hidden Truth

Wealth is not something you pursue.
It's something you stabilize within your field.

You've been taught to chase outcomes.
The wealthy — knowingly or not — maintain these laws as their baseline.

Now that you've seen them, you are no longer blind to why hustle has failed you — and why alignment will free you.

Daily Ritual: Alignment Script + Wealth Trigger Journal

"You don't hold alignment once. You return to it daily."

Knowing the laws is not enough.
Embodiment is repetition.
This ritual gives you a system to tune your wealth field every morning and calibrate your alignment as you operate.

PART 1 — The Alignment Script

Every morning, before action or decision-making, speak this script aloud:

"I am safe with wealth.
My field holds expansion without fear.
I am not becoming someone. I am remembering who I am.
My signal is clean. My decisions are clear.
I compress value into every move.
I release the need for external permission.
I move from calibration, not compensation.
My visibility is precise. My presence is magnetic.
Wealth is not outside of me. Wealth responds to what I hold."

How to use it:

- Stand tall. Shoulders open. Breath steady.

- Speak slowly, like issuing commands to your field — not like reading a quote.

- If any line feels "off" inside you, pause and feel where your nervous system resists. That's your next layer of work.

Optional Upgrade:
Add 1 personal line each week that addresses your current edge:
"I now release _____. I now hold _____."

PART 2 — The Wealth Trigger Journal

Every evening, you close your day by running a short audit that reinforces your alignment and exposes hidden distortions before they calcify.

3 Daily Journal Prompts:

1. Where did I act from alignment today?
(Where did I hold my standard, price, boundary, visibility, or focus?)

2. Where did I feel the pull to hustle, overcompensate, or self-doubt?
(Identify the triggers — not with shame, but with clarity.)

3. What calibration can I make tomorrow?
(One micro-shift to bring the field back into coherence.)

This is your daily wealth hygiene. The game is not perfection — it's **awareness, adjustment, and authority.**

Why This Ritual Works

- The **morning script** programs your identity and nervous system before external chaos can touch you.

- The **evening journal** allows you to track your real patterns, not your intentions.

- Over days and weeks, you'll see your alignment stabilize, your decisions sharpen, and your income pathways multiply — because you are becoming the person who holds wealth by law, not effort.

The Alignment Rehearsal

After your evening journal, close your eyes and choose one moment where you acted out of alignment today.

See the scene.
Feel where your nervous system pulled you off course.
Now, rewind the moment — but this time, move through it aligned.

Visualize:

- Your posture: calm, grounded, certain.

- Your voice: clear, unapologetic.

- Your decision: holding your standard.

- Your emotions: neutral, unattached to the outcome.

Watch how the conversation, negotiation, pricing, or action plays out differently.

Why this works:
You're not just reviewing — you're rehearsing the aligned version of you. This gives your body a **reference point** to draw from the next time you face a similar situation.

The nervous system doesn't change from theory.
It changes from felt repetition.
Visualization creates felt safety for the identity you're building.

Protocol III is now complete.
You have purged. You have tuned. You have aligned.
Now you begin to build.

PART II — The Tactical Protocols: Systems, Income & Visibility

You've cleared the parasites.
You've tuned your frequency.
You've aligned your identity to wealth.

Now, we shift into **external architecture.**

Wealth is not sustained through energy alone.
It must be housed inside systems.

Most people try to build systems from scarcity:

- Budgeting from fear

- Overcomplicating their offers

- Chasing audiences without alignment

- Hustling for visibility without energetic authority

This part is where you break that cycle.

- You will build **income flows** that match your energetic capacity.

- You will design **offers** that compress value and scale without burnout.

- You will establish **visibility protocols** that magnetize wealth through precision, not noise.

You don't need a complicated business model.
You need a clean, scalable wealth engine built from alignment.

This part of the book is not about "financial advice."
It's about **wealth infrastructure** — designed for freelancers, consultants, creatives, healers, employees, or entrepreneurs.

Your work may be spiritual.
Your systems must still be structural.

Part II is where form meets field.

Now, we build.

Protocol IV — The Wealth Flow Map

How to Split Your Income into Clear, Intentional Streams

Wealth is not just about how much you earn.
It's about how you **move** what you earn.

Money without structure dissolves.
Money with clarity multiplies.

Most people don't struggle because they're incapable of earning.
They struggle because their money flows are chaotic, undefined, and emotionally reactive.

- They mix personal and business finances.

- They overspend without knowing where their actual capacity is.

- They trap themselves in income cycles that feel busy but aren't scalable.

- They make every dollar carry too many jobs — safety, survival, guilt, desire.

The problem isn't lack of money — it's **lack of flow design.**

The Energetic Trap of Undefined Money

Every time money enters your life without a clear assignment, your nervous system scrambles:

- Should I save this?

- Should I spend it?

- Should I invest?

- Should I hold onto it out of fear?

53

- What if more doesn't come?

This constant micro-anxiety leads to:

- Hoarding energy

- Panic spending

- Guilt-based generosity

- Cycles of feast and famine

The wealthy don't operate this way.
They don't emotionally negotiate every dollar.
They **pre-decide** where money flows — before it arrives.

The Wealth Flow Map: Your Financial Nervous System

The **Wealth Flow Map** is your energetic stabilizer.
It tells your field: *We know where money belongs.*

It works because:

- It removes emotional chaos.

- It gives every dollar a job.

- It aligns your financial structure to your energetic expansion.

- It makes your income scalable because your system is ready to hold more.

You're not "managing money" — you're building **flow architecture**.

The 5 Core Streams

These aren't bank accounts.
These are **energetic containers** your system will recognize and stabilize.

1. **Essentials** — Survival & Stability

- Rent/mortgage

- Bills, groceries, transportation

- Baseline peace

2. **Expansion** — Wealth Creation

- Business growth

- Investments

- Education that expands capacity

3. **Enjoyment** — Joyful Wealth Circulation

- Travel

- Experiences

- Upgrades that support your identity shift

4. **Reserves** — Safety & Calm

- Emergency fund

- Unexpected expenses

- Cash buffer (not hoarding, but stability)

5. **Generosity** — Aligned Giving

- Donations

- Family support (without guilt obligation)

- Contribution that feels sovereign

The Flow Principle:

When money has a clear job, your nervous system relaxes.
When your nervous system relaxes, your field expands.
When your field expands, your income rises.

Most people try to make more first.
The wealthy design flow first — so when more comes, it sticks.

Start Simple

You don't need 5 new accounts today. You need clarity first. The structure will follow.

- Define your current percentages for each stream (even if your income feels small right now).

- As your income grows, maintain the flow map — not just your survival thinking.

- Even if you're earning $500/month or $50,000/month — the structure remains.

You're not here to juggle money.
You're here to **stabilize wealth flows your field can easily hold.**

How to Structure Your 3–5 Digital Accounts for Clarity, Purpose, and Scalability

Now that you've designed your Wealth Flow Map, it's time to give your money a home.
This is where you move from energetic clarity into physical containment — without overwhelm.
You will grow into this system as your income expands.

The Wealth Flow Map gave your money purpose.
Now we give it **structure.**

Energetic clarity without physical containment leads to leakage.
Physical containment without energetic clarity leads to stagnation.
You need both.

Most people operate with one checking account, one credit card, and a fog of emotional decisions layered on top of undefined balances.

This system will end that.

The Principle of Separation

Every dollar should know its role.
Every account should hold one job.

When you separate your flows into distinct digital containers:

- You eliminate emotional decision-making.

- You see exactly where you stand in every area.

- You reduce mental clutter around money.

- You stabilize your nervous system — because uncertainty evaporates.

The goal isn't to make your finances complicated.
The goal is to make them **visible, organized, and scalable.**

The 3–5 Account Structure

Depending on your current situation, you'll build between 3 and 5 digital accounts (or sub-accounts inside your banking platform if available).

These align directly with your Wealth Flow Map.

1. Operations Account (Essentials)

- Rent, utilities, groceries, transportation, subscriptions

- The day-to-day stability of your financial life

- This account holds your safety and peace

2. Expansion Account (Growth)

- Business expenses, marketing, education, investments, coaching

- Every dollar here is fueling future wealth

- This account activates forward movement

3. Enjoyment Account (Lifestyle)

- Travel, experiences, personal upgrades

- This ensures you are embodying wealth, not hoarding it

- Joy expands your capacity to receive

4. Reserves Account (Safety Net)

- Emergency fund, large upcoming expenses, unexpected needs

- This is your stabilization buffer — not your fear-based hoarding pile

- Calm creates better financial decisions

---

5. Generosity Account (Giving)

- Donations, family support, aligned contributions

- This keeps your wealth circulation clean and intentional

- Giving from sovereignty, not guilt, strengthens your field

Why This Works (Energetically and Practically)

- You no longer wonder "Can I afford this?" — you look at the container.

- You stop collapsing business and personal finances into chaos.

- You create natural boundaries that prevent self-sabotage.

- Your income becomes **organized energy**, not emotional noise.

Money loves order.
The clearer your containment, the easier wealth flows.

Start Where You Are

- If you're starting from scratch, even 3 accounts can stabilize your system immediately:

  o Essentials

  o Expansion

  o Reserves

- As your income grows, you can add the full 5-stream model.

- Many online banks and financial platforms allow you to open multiple sub-accounts for free. Use them.

This isn't complexity — this is command.

Tool: Create Your Personalized Money Flow Grid

"When your wealth has a map, your nervous system can finally relax."

This is where clarity becomes command.
You've designed your Wealth Flow Map.
You've structured your physical accounts.
Now you create your **Money Flow Grid** — your living, personal blueprint.

Most people's finances feel chaotic because everything floats in abstraction:

- "I make about this much..."

- "I think I can afford it..."

- "I'll figure it out when I get paid..."

The Grid removes that fog completely.

What The Money Flow Grid Does:

- Shows you exactly where your income goes — before it even arrives.

- Aligns your spending with your energetic expansion.

- Prevents emotional financial decisions.

- Keeps your system scalable as income rises.

- Creates **instant financial sovereignty.**

Step 1 — Define Your Current Monthly Income

- This includes salary, freelance work, business income, side hustles, or any active money streams.

- Don't inflate or estimate — start with reality.

Clarity begins with what's real, not what's ideal.

Step 2 — Apply Your Flow Percentages

For each Wealth Stream (based on your 3–5 account structure), assign a percentage of your total income.

Here's a starting model for many people:

Wealth Stream	Suggested Allocation
Essentials (Operations)	50–60%
Expansion (Growth)	10–20%
Enjoyment (Lifestyle)	10–15%
Reserves (Safety Net)	10–15%
Generosity (Giving)	5–10%

These are not rules — they are templates.
Your unique life phase will shape your exact numbers.

Step 3 — Input Your Numbers

Now multiply your income by each percentage to see your **exact monthly allocations**.

Example (Monthly Income: $5,000):

Wealth Stream	Allocation	Amount
Essentials	55%	$2,750
Expansion	15%	$750
Enjoyment	10%	$500
Reserves	15%	$750
Generosity	5%	$250

Step 4 — Audit and Adjust

- Do these numbers feel sustainable?

- Are any areas currently over-extended or neglected?

- Where can you start realigning gently without stress?

This is a recalibration tool — not a judgment system.

If your current reality is heavily weighted toward survival, your first goal is to stabilize Essentials — while still feeding small amounts into Expansion, Reserves, and Enjoyment.

Even allocating **$10 to Reserves** each month activates sovereignty. Even setting aside **$20 into Expansion** sends a signal to your field:

I am building capacity.

Step 5 — Install The Grid Physically

- Use your digital accounts to house each stream.

- Automate transfers on payday.

- The goal: **make financial movement automatic, not emotional.**

Every dollar knows where it belongs.
Your nervous system knows where you stand.
Your field knows how to scale safely.

The Money Flow Grid is not about control.
It's about removing distortion.
It's about giving your wealth a structure worthy of your expansion.

Protocol V — Energy-Proofing Your Financial Life

Find Where Your Money "Leaks" and How to Seal It

Wealth isn't only about how much you bring in.
It's also about how much you unconsciously bleed out.

You're not always under-earning.
You're often over-leaking.

Most people never realize where their energy and money are quietly slipping away, not because they're reckless — but because the leaks are **invisible, habitual, and emotional.**

Before you scale further, you must seal these leaks — otherwise, you'll keep filling a bucket with a hole in the bottom.

What Is a Money Leak?

A money leak is any unconscious outflow of financial, emotional, or energetic resources that:

- Doesn't create real value

- Isn't aligned with your current identity

- Feeds old patterns of safety, guilt, or avoidance

- Weakens your field of sovereignty

The 4 Types of Wealth Leaks

1. Emotional Leaks

- Spending to soothe anxiety, not to expand identity

- "Rewarding yourself" for surviving — while still feeling financially unstable

- Guilt-driven generosity: giving because you feel obligated, not sovereign

- Rescuing others financially to avoid discomfort

Emotional leaks weaken your boundaries — and create invisible resentment.

---

2. Attention Leaks

- Subscriptions you forgot to cancel

- Services you no longer use

- Platforms you pay for but rarely touch

- Courses you bought but never implemented

Attention leaks often disguise themselves as "opportunities" — but drain your focus and finances slowly over time.

---

3. Structural Leaks

- Mixing personal and business expenses

- Disorganized account structures

- Undefined payment cycles

- Random debt stacking without conscious plan

Structural leaks don't feel emotional — but they constantly produce background anxiety that drains clarity.

---

4. Identity Leaks

- Holding onto expenses that match your *past self*, not your current trajectory

- Maintaining lifestyles, memberships, or relationships that no longer align with your future field

- Fear of upgrading or releasing what no longer fits your energetic identity

Every time you fund an expired version of yourself, you delay your expansion.

Why Energy Leaks Multiply

Leaks compound invisibly.
One small subscription becomes twenty.
One fear-driven gift becomes habitual enabling.
One identity expense becomes an entire lifestyle of outdated obligations.

The result?

- Diminished financial clarity

- Emotional resentment

- Subtle energetic burnout

- Loss of momentum

Wealth requires containment.
If your field is leaking, your scaling will always feel heavy.

The Energetic Law Behind It:

Money respects sovereignty.
Leaks signal self-abandonment.

The more contained your field, the more trust your wealth system holds.

Panic Spending vs Power Spending

You don't just spend money.
You project energy through it.

Every financial decision carries a frequency.
And that frequency either stabilizes your field or fractures it.

Most people aren't overspending because they're irresponsible.
They're overspending because they've never been taught to differentiate between:

- **Panic Spending:** reactive, distorted, driven by fear, emptiness, or emotional bypassing

- **Power Spending:** intentional, sovereign, driven by identity, clarity, and energetic expansion

---

Panic Spending — The Hidden Saboteur

Panic spending doesn't always look like shopping sprees.
It's far more subtle — and dangerous:

- Buying courses, tools, or coaching out of desperation to "finally fix it"

- Shopping to self-soothe anxiety or reward yourself for surviving

- Over-gifting to avoid guilt or family tension

- Upgrading environments or brands prematurely to *prove* you're evolving

- Making offers or business moves driven by fear of being irrelevant or behind

Panic spending is the nervous system trying to regulate through consumption — but never actually feeling safer.

The pattern looks like:

Fear → Spend → Temporary Relief → Guilt → More Fear

Power Spending — The Field Multiplier

Power spending feels completely different:

- Purchases aligned with your expansion timeline

- Investments that amplify your capabilities, not your insecurities

- Spending that reflects the identity you are *becoming*

- Decisions made from spaciousness, not urgency

- Contributions that flow from abundance, not obligation

Power spending expands your field because it's rooted in stability.

The pattern looks like:

Clarity → Invest → Ownership → Expansion → Stability

The Core Difference:

	Panic Spending	Power Spending
Emotion	Fear, lack, avoidance	Clarity, sovereignty, expansion
Timing	Reactive	Intentional
Nervous System	Dysregulated	Grounded
Outcome	Guilt, instability	Growth, stability
Energetic Message	"I'm not enough."	"I am aligned."

The Energetic Filter:

Before any significant financial decision, ask yourself:

"Is this feeding my nervous system or my expansion?"
"Is this regulating my fear or activating my next level?"

Your answer will tell you exactly which frequency you're operating from.

True wealth is not restrictive.
But it is always sovereign.

You don't need to stop spending.
You need to spend with the field you're building — not the fear you're running from.

Simple Ways to Remove Energetic Leaks: Subscriptions, Debt Cycles, Toxic Transactions

**Every leak you tolerate is a silent contract with scarcity.
Cancelling is not loss — it's reclamation.**

Wealth isn't always blocked by the big decisions.
Often, it's slowly drained by **small, consistent leaks** you've stopped noticing.

These aren't just financial decisions.
They're energetic agreements you're still unconsciously signing.

Let's break down the three core leak zones:

---

1. Subscriptions — The "Silent Drip" Leaks

In most modern lives, subscriptions have become **unconscious commitments:**

- Software you no longer use

- Platforms you signed up for but never integrated

- Coaching memberships you feel guilty leaving

- Apps that charge monthly fees for services you forgot existed

- Duplicate services offering the same function

Energetic Cost:

- Each one splits your attention and dilutes your sovereignty.

- Every tiny withdrawal reinforces "I don't have full clarity over my flow."

- Subconscious anxiety rises because your field doesn't fully trust your management.

72

Purge Principle:

If it's not actively contributing to your income, identity upgrade, or spiritual expansion — release it.

- Audit every subscription across personal, business, and lifestyle categories.

- Set a hard rule: **One decision = one frequency.**

- Unsubscribe with ceremony:

"I release what no longer amplifies my expansion. I close this contract now."

---

2. Debt Cycles — The "Future Drain" Leaks

Debt isn't inherently bad.
But unresolved or reactive debt locks you into **future scarcity loops.**

Where debt becomes energetically toxic:

- High-interest consumer debt (credit cards, loans) that were used for emotional regulation, not strategic growth

- Fear-driven refinancing without addressing spending patterns

- Multiple scattered debt sources with no clear payoff plan

- Carrying balances that create background dread every month

Energetic Cost:

- Chronic anxiety

- Subtle shame

- Nervous system activation every time a bill appears

- Identity entanglement with being "behind" or "in survival"

Purge Principle:

Face every dollar you owe.
Clarity dissolves distortion.

- List every debt with full transparency: total, interest rate, minimum payments.

- Prioritize repayment not emotionally, but strategically:

    o High-interest first.

    o Small victories next (quick payoffs).

- Design a simple **Debt Purge Plan** that activates relief — not more pressure.

"I choose visibility over avoidance. I neutralize these drains with structure."

---

3. Toxic Transactions — The "Identity Loop" Leaks

These are the most insidious, because they often feel emotionally noble:

- Financial enabling of others to maintain peace or control

- Obligatory family contributions rooted in guilt or generational programming

- Business collaborations where money leaks into unequal partnerships

- Over-delivering for clients far beyond your energetic agreement

Energetic Cost:

- Identity confusion

- Emotional depletion

- Loss of authority in your wealth field

- Resentment cycles that destabilize your aura

Purge Principle:

You don't owe your past or anyone else your financial sovereignty.

- Audit your recurring "obligation payments" — both personal and professional.

- Set clear policies for boundaries, pricing, and support moving forward.

- Release enmeshments with grace:

"I can love them and honor my field simultaneously."

The Hidden Truth

Every leak you seal sends a signal:
"I am no longer available for disorganized wealth."

The goal isn't restriction — it's clarity.
The clearer your containment, the more confidently wealth enters your system.

Practice — The 7-Day Financial Cleanse + Awareness Tracker

"You don't need more discipline. You need less distortion."

You've seen where your leaks live.
Now it's time to begin **the purge**.

This is not just financial housekeeping.
This is **energetic sovereignty work**.
Every leak you close reinforces your wealth field's structural integrity.

Wealth isn't built by force.
It's stabilized by containment.

The Purpose of This Cleanse

- Remove subtle energetic leaks.

- Recalibrate your relationship with spending and containment.

- Reset your nervous system's sense of financial stability.

- Prepare your system to hold larger amounts of income without fear.

The 7-Day Cleanse Process

DAY 1 — The Full Exposure

Goal:
Bring every hidden leak into full visibility.

Actions:

- Pull your last 90 days of bank statements, credit card transactions, and PayPal or business payment platforms.

- Create a simple 3-column sheet:

  o *Necessary | Useful | Leak*

Necessary: Required for current stability (rent, bills, etc.)
Useful: Actively contributes to growth, expansion, or identity building
Leak: Emotional, outdated, fear-driven, or unconscious expenses

- Don't justify. Don't edit. Just classify.

DAY 2 — Subscription Audit

Goal:
Eliminate attention leaks.

Actions:

- Cancel every subscription or recurring payment in the "Leak" column.

- If any feel emotionally charged, use the declaration:

"I release this drain. I choose aligned containment."

- Keep only what actively supports your identity expansion.

DAY 3 — Toxic Transaction Audit

Goal:
Identify emotionally enmeshed money drains.

Actions:

- List every person, partnership, or obligation where you are spending from guilt, fear, or avoidance.

- For each one, write:

    o *How much?*

    o *Why am I continuing this?*

    o *Is this aligned with my next-level identity?*

- Begin planning **graceful exits or restructured agreements**.

DAY 4 — Debt Neutralization

Goal:
Face your full debt position with sovereignty.

Actions:

- List each debt: total owed, interest rate, payment frequency.

- Prioritize repayment:

    o High-interest first.

    o Quick wins next.

- Build a **simple Debt Purge Plan**: dates, amounts, targets.

This removes the energetic fog.
You control the debt now — it no longer controls you.

DAY 5 — Micro-Spending Awareness

Goal:
Interrupt small leaks that accumulate.

Actions:

- For one full day, track **every single dollar spent** — no matter how small.

- At night, review:

  - Was this power spending or panic spending?

  - Did this expand or contract my field?

This builds **conscious wealth reflexes**.

DAY 6 — Identity Leak Audit

Goal:
Eliminate expenses that still reflect who you *used to be* — even after you've removed the obvious subscriptions.

This is where you confront not what you forgot — but what you're still emotionally attached to.

Actions:

- Review your lifestyle and spending through the lens of your **next-level identity**.

- Look for:

  - Outdated professional memberships you maintain out of habit or fear of "falling behind"

  - Lifestyle choices that no longer feel aligned but serve to project an image

  - Status purchases designed to signal worth or belonging

  - Business expenses tied to old positioning, niches, or offers you've outgrown

- Ask yourself:

  o "Is this supporting the person I'm building into — or keeping me tied to the version I'm outgrowing?"

- Begin phasing these out immediately and consciously.

Declare:
"I fund my current identity, not my past programming."

DAY 7 — The Containment Command

Goal:
Seal the purge. Stabilize the field.

Actions:

- Sit in silence. Close your eyes.

- Speak aloud or internally:

"I have closed the leaks.
I hold my wealth field clean.
No energy exits without conscious command.
I am safe with expansion.
I am trusted to hold more."

- Breathe deeply and visualize your Money Flow Grid glowing — fully contained.

Daily Awareness Tracker (Use Daily Through The Cleanse)

Every night, answer:

1. What leak did I close or confront today?
2. What emotion arose as I released it?
3. How did my body respond after the purge?
4. Where am I becoming more sovereign?

The Truth:

You don't attract more by forcing. You attract more by proving you can contain.

The cleaner your field, the louder your wealth signal becomes.

Protocol VI — Magnetic Wealth Creation (Without Overwhelm)

Build Your First Scalable Offer from What You Already Know

You were programmed to believe that creating wealth means creating endless complexity:

- New certifications

- Perfect offers

- Massive audiences

- Aggressive sales funnels

That's a lie.

Wealth creation begins when you **simplify your knowledge into value loops** that serve others and stabilize your income — without compromising your energy.

You don't need to "be ready."
You need to **extract what you already carry** and build from there.

Why Most People Stay Stuck at "I'm Not Ready Yet"

The mind tells stories:

- *"I need more experience."*

- *"I need a bigger audience."*

- *"I need better branding."*

- *"I'm not certified enough yet."*

These aren't truths.
They're parasite programs disguised as "professionalism."

The real block is **nervous system resistance to visibility, pricing, and energetic containment**.

Wealth doesn't respond to how perfect your offer is.
It responds to **how cleanly you hold your field while offering it**.

The Magnetic Wealth Principle:

You don't monetize what you learn.
You monetize what you've embodied.

- People pay for your ability to simplify what they're stuck in.

- People are drawn to your clarity — not your complexity.

- People want to borrow your stabilized field — not your information overload.

Extracting Your First Scalable Offer

The fastest way to start wealth creation without overwhelm is to ask:

Where am I 3–5 steps ahead of someone else?

Not 30 steps. Not a guru.
Just far enough ahead to hold clean clarity for others.

You can monetize:

- A skill you've mastered through repetition

- A process you've simplified from your own experience

- A solution you've lived through and resolved

- A system you've created in your personal, business, or spiritual life

You Already Carry an Offer

Your income lives inside your field — not inside another certification.

Examples:

- The freelancer who mastered pricing and boundaries → teaches others to do the same.

- The holistic coach who healed burnout → creates a 6-week energy stabilization program.

- The remote worker who built client systems → designs a consulting offer for other service providers.

- The employee who learned to negotiate raises → builds a salary negotiation coaching product.

The Key to Scalability

We're not building a job.
We're building a **small, scalable value loop**:

- Simple offer → Delivered cleanly → Repeatable structure → Contained energetics

When you simplify your value into **repeatable delivery**, you free your time, stabilize your field, and amplify your income.

This is not "build an empire."
This is **build a self-contained wealth circuit** that grows as your capacity grows.

Design a Small, Scalable Value Loop (a.k.a. *Money Mirror*) — Deepened Version

---

What You're About to Build

**Wealth is not created by adding more work.
It's created by building repeatable loops that stabilize your energy while serving others.**

Most people stay broke because they keep exchanging hours for dollars:

- One client. One transaction. One temporary result.

That pattern constantly resets your nervous system into hustle, anxiety, and financial uncertainty.

A **Value Loop** is different.
You're not chasing random money.
You're building a **contained offer system** that:

- Extracts what you already carry.

- Packages it into repeatable transformations.

- Serves your clients with clarity.

- Stabilizes your income without draining your nervous system.

This is your first step into **magnetic, scalable wealth.**

First: The Core Shift You Must Understand

Every dollar that will ever enter your life arrives through one truth:

Money moves to those who solve problems others cannot solve for themselves.

Whether you're a coach, designer, freelancer, consultant, healer, or builder of any kind — **you get paid to resolve friction for others.**

Friction = stuckness, confusion, pain, fear, or limitation.

You do not need to be perfect.
You only need to be 3–5 steps ahead of the people you serve — holding clarity they haven't stabilized yet.

The 4 Core Components of Your Value Loop (Fully Expanded)

---

1. The Pain You Resolve — Why People Pay

Nobody pays for information.
They pay to move out of pain.
They pay to collapse confusion into clarity.

All money is a transaction of emotional relief.

No matter your field, you're relieving friction:

- A burned-out entrepreneur pays for clear time systems.

- A frustrated freelancer pays to fix pricing and boundaries.

- A spiritually exhausted person pays to reconnect with energy and confidence.

- A confused beginner pays to collapse years of mistakes into a simple process.

Your job is not to impress. Your job is to resolve.

If you don't know your client's pain, your offer will always feel foggy. The clearer you see their struggle, the faster your offer sells — because they feel seen.

2. The Process You Deliver — How You Create Movement

You are not selling hours.
You are selling clarity — packaged into steps.

Here's where most people get lost. They believe they need some massive complicated method.
You don't.

- Look at your own journey.

- Where did you used to be stuck?

- What simple sequence helped you shift?

Your process might be:

- 3 key decisions

- 5 core tools

- 4-step audit

- A phased timeline

Your process exists to move people from stuck → stable.

The simpler and clearer, the better.

You're not teaching everything you know.
You're walking them across the bridge you've already crossed.

---

3. The Format You Deliver — How Your Energy Stays Clean

Here's where most people burn out:

- They offer everything to everyone.

- No clear structure.

- No container to protect their time or focus.

Your delivery format must match your energetic capacity.

You are not building an empire here.
You're building **containment** — a clean delivery system that allows your nervous system to remain stable while your income flows.

Formats you can choose from:

- **1:1 Sessions (Fixed Package):**
  Ideal for those starting with minimal audience. You serve a set number of clients at a high level of personalization — but with clear boundaries and timelines.

- **Small Group Cohorts:**
  You serve multiple people simultaneously, teaching the same process, while preserving your energy through leveraged teaching.

- **Workshops & Intensives:**
  Short, focused sessions that create transformation in a condensed timeframe, without committing you to ongoing endless support.

- **Digital Products:**
  Once you refine your process, you can scale it into recorded trainings, workbooks, templates, or full self-study courses.

Containment rule:
The format you choose must feel **spacious, sustainable, and repeatable.**

- If your offer feels heavy — you won't sell it.

- If your offer feels clean — your field will pull clients toward it.

4. The Containment Rule — How You Hold Wealth

Containment is what makes your income scalable.

Most people design offers that immediately drain their nervous system:

- Open-ended coaching

- Unlimited revisions

- Constant access

- No boundaries on time or scope

When you create offers without clear containment, you unconsciously avoid selling — because your nervous system senses the overwhelm.

Containment is not restriction — it's authority.

Your offer needs:

- Clear start and end points

- Defined deliverables

- Limited access points

- Simple fulfillment

Example:

"You'll go through my 4-step pricing reset. 4 weekly calls. Private audit. Access to a group chat during the program. Then we close the container."

The tighter your offer's boundaries, the stronger your field feels holding it.

When your offer feels light, your sales flow naturally.

Why This Model Is Called The *Money Mirror*

Because what you build reflects the same energetic structure we've already been designing:

- Parasite Purge → you cleared distortion.

- Frequency Recode → you stabilized your signal.

- Flow Map → you structured your income streams.

- Financial Cleanse → you sealed your leaks.

Now, your offer itself must mirror that same **clarity, structure, and sovereignty.**

The way you design your income container is a direct mirror of how you now hold your energetic field.

Transform What You Know Into Something That Pays You

Your wealth is trapped inside unorganized clarity. Extraction releases it.

The offer you're meant to build isn't hiding somewhere outside of you. It's already encoded in your experience, your past struggles, and the clarity you've stabilized.

This extraction ritual helps you pull it out of potential and into form.

The Extraction Sequence

Excellent. You're absolutely right — this is where we make the book **land inside their actual reality.** Otherwise it risks sounding like theoretical coaching advice (which is *exactly* what we're avoiding).

Let's go step-by-step and add real, diverse examples across fields, industries, and life paths — not just online business.

Step 1 — The Personal Inventory (Expanded with Examples)

Sit with full honesty. Write these out by hand:

---

1. Where have I personally experienced the most transformation in my life, work, or skills?

Examples:

- I went from constantly being in debt to building a simple, automated financial system.

- I healed my chronic fatigue through specific nutritional protocols.

91

- I mastered setting boundaries with toxic family dynamics.

- I turned my hobby of photography into a consistent part-time income.

- I negotiated multiple salary raises without needing new credentials.

- I transitioned from a corporate job into freelance consulting while keeping my income stable.

---

2. What patterns have I mastered that others still struggle with?

Examples:

- Pricing services with confidence (freelancers, designers, consultants).

- Structuring offers that don't require endless customization (coaches, service providers).

- Managing personal anxiety while under high performance pressure (executives, athletes).

- Creating visibility for a local healing practice without burning out (yoga teachers, holistic practitioners).

- Organizing a household with multiple children and careers (parents, working mothers).

- Simplifying complex spiritual teachings into practical daily rituals (healers, energy workers).

---

3. What processes do people already ask me for help with?

Examples:

- Friends asking how I save and invest while earning a modest salary.

- Coworkers asking for help preparing for job interviews and salary negotiations.

- Family asking for meal plans to balance energy naturally.

- Other freelancers asking how I get repeat clients without paid ads.

- Clients asking for guidance on clearing emotional blocks before public speaking.

- Entrepreneurs asking how I structure my daily workflow to avoid burnout.

---

4. Where do I feel unshakeably clear?

Examples:

- I know exactly how to create an easy system for someone overwhelmed by money.

- I feel clear teaching new freelancers how to price themselves.

- I feel at peace guiding people to set energetic boundaries with family.

- I feel strong showing someone how to negotiate higher rates or salaries.

- I feel deeply grounded when teaching breathwork or daily rituals for nervous system regulation.

- I feel clear explaining how to simplify daily business operations without tech overwhelm.

Key Reminder:
You are not trying to invent something.
You are locating the clarity you already embody that others would pay for to collapse their learning curve.

Step 2 — The Friction Scan (Continued and Completed)

For each area you identified, you continue to clarify:
What problem does it solve? Where are they stuck? How is it costing them?

We'll go broader now — pulling examples from multiple industries, life paths, and spiritual domains to make it feel fully applicable.

Health, Energy & Wellness Examples

- They're exhausted but overwhelmed by conflicting nutrition advice.

- They feel trapped in cycles of starting and quitting exercise routines.

- They struggle with chronic stress and can't calm their nervous system.

- They've tried multiple healing modalities but haven't integrated them into daily life.

- They carry emotional eating patterns they feel powerless to shift.

Cost: Ongoing fatigue, burnout, health instability, lost confidence in their body.

Career & Salary Negotiation Examples

- They're underpaid but terrified to ask for a raise.

- They're doing more than their role but can't advocate for promotion.

- They freeze in job interviews and feel inarticulate.

- They've applied for dozens of jobs with no response due to weak resumes.

- They doubt they're "qualified enough" to transition careers.

Cost: Financial stagnation, career frustration, internalized imposter syndrome.

Freelance, Consulting & Creative Work Examples

- They're constantly discounting their services to land clients.

- They don't know how to create package offers instead of hourly work.

- They have no client onboarding systems, leading to chaotic delivery.

- They fear saying "no" to bad-fit clients, so they stay overloaded.

- They don't know how to market without feeling fake or desperate.

Cost: Income volatility, creative burnout, client boundary stress, undercharging.

Spiritual & Emotional Sovereignty Examples

- They crave purpose but feel spiritually scattered.

- They keep returning to the same emotional wounds without fully clearing them.

- They feel blocked from manifestation but don't know why.

- They rely on endless healing modalities without creating real-world shifts.

- They seek energetic sovereignty but remain hooked into validation loops.

Cost: Stuck energy, emotional depletion, spiritual frustration, blocked wealth.

Family, Parenting & Relationship Examples

- They struggle to set boundaries with demanding family members.

- They feel pulled between parenting, work, and self-care with no structure.

- They enable others financially out of guilt or obligation.

- They avoid hard conversations, allowing resentment to build silently.

- They fear outgrowing loved ones if they pursue wealth or personal growth.

Cost: Emotional exhaustion, guilt-driven decisions, drained financial and energetic reserves.

Local & Offline Business Examples

- They run a physical business but feel overwhelmed managing operations.

- They struggle to hire or delegate because no systems exist.

- They underprice services because they feel guilty charging locally.

- They're afraid to raise rates in tight-knit communities.

- They avoid marketing or visibility, believing "word of mouth is enough."

Cost: Plateaus in income, emotional burnout, trapped in unscalable operations.

The Friction Scan is the heartbeat of offer clarity.

The more precisely you articulate the friction your offer resolves, the more **magnetic** your message becomes — because your client feels: *"That's exactly where I'm stuck."*

KEY REMINDER:

This is not about niching down into a tiny box.
This is about **honoring where you already hold stabilized clarity** for others to access.

Step 3 — The Process Download

Now extract the *pathway* you've already walked.

For each solution:

- Break it into 3–5 clear steps.

- Keep it simple.

- Avoid overwhelming theory.

- Focus on the core decisions, tools, or actions that move them from **stuck → stable.**

If you overcomplicate this, you're building a drain.
Simplicity is what your field — and your clients — can stabilize.

Step 4 — The Format Decision

Choose your **current containment**:

- Do you want to deliver this 1:1 first?

- Can this be run as a small group?

- Could you host a live intensive?

- Are you ready for a simple digital version?

Choose what your nervous system can hold **right now**, not what impresses others.

You build higher leverage later.
You start with clean containment now.

Step 5 — The Pricing Anchor

Now price your offer.

Use this principle:

Price at the number where your body feels both slightly stretched but still sovereign.

- If it feels too low — you'll resent your work.

- If it feels too high — you'll energetically collapse while selling.

You're not pricing your worth.
You're pricing the clarity, confidence, and value stability you transfer to others.

Start here. You will expand pricing as your nervous system stabilizes with delivery.

Step 6 — The Offer Declaration
This is your first energetic contract.

Write your offer in one clear sentence:

"I help [who] go from [current stuck state] to [desired clarity] through [your process] delivered via [your format] for [$X price]."

Examples:

- *I help overwhelmed freelancers go from pricing anxiety to confident premium rates through my 4-step pricing blueprint, delivered via a 4-week small group coaching program, priced at $1,200.*

- *I help burned-out mothers go from chronic fatigue to energetic stability through my 3-phase daily ritual system, delivered as a digital self-study course, priced at $297.*

- *I help new consultants go from scattered offers to scalable packages through my signature 5-step offer design intensive, delivered via a live weekend workshop, priced at $2,500.*

Clarity creates energetic containment.
Containment creates confidence.
Confidence creates magnetism.

When you declare your offer in this way, your nervous system receives a clear blueprint:
This is what I am offering. This is who I serve. This is how I serve them.

Your mind no longer needs to constantly renegotiate your business model. Your field holds the structure.

Final Energetic Command:

Stand or sit grounded.
Speak aloud:

"I release the story that I need more to begin.
I stabilize what I already carry.
My field is ready to hold this offer.
My wealth structure begins now."

Pause.
Breathe.
Feel the stability of this decision settle into your system.

Ritual: Launch Your Money Magnet Project

Wealth doesn't respond to thought.
Wealth responds to transmission.

You've extracted your offer.
You've stabilized your structure.
Now it must leave your private mind and enter public reality.

This is not a launch.
This is an **energetic command.**

Why This Ritual Exists

Most people stay trapped for years in the "preparation phase" because:

- They overthink their audience.

- They fear being judged.

- They wait for perfect conditions.

- They get lost in overbuilding, branding, and tech.

Perfection is a delay mechanism for nervous system safety.

The only way to fully stabilize your wealth field is to **make the offer visible.**

Not theoretical.
Not "in progress."
Visible.

The Law of the Field Activation

Money responds to exposure.
Exposure stabilizes clarity.
Clarity attracts clients.

Until your offer exists outside of your head, your nervous system holds energetic ambiguity.
Visibility collapses the ambiguity.

You no longer *hope* you're building something.
You *are* building something — because others can see it, respond to it, and enter your field.

The 72-Hour Activation Sequence

You will move into visible offer creation within 72 hours.
No delay. No spiraling. No perfectionism.

DAY 1 — The Public Declaration

Post publicly in whatever platform or medium feels most natural:

- Social media

- Personal network

- Email list

- Local community

Your message must contain:

- Who you serve

- What problem you help solve

- How you deliver it

- Your call to action

Example Post:
"I'm opening 3 spots for freelancers who feel stuck undercharging their services.
In 4 weeks, I help you break the pricing fear loop, install clean client

102

boundaries, and stabilize your income with confidence.
This is delivered through weekly private sessions with full pricing audits.
If you're ready, message me to apply."

Energetic Command:

"I am safe being seen.
My offer holds value.
My visibility holds power."

DAY 2 — The Direct Outreach

Privately reach out to 3–5 people who:

- Have shown past interest.

- Are likely ideal clients.

- Are close to your energetic circle.

This is not begging or convincing.
This is offering an aligned solution you confidently hold.

Example Outreach:
"Hey [Name], I'm offering a focused 4-week container for freelancers
struggling with pricing clarity.
I thought of you because I know you've been navigating this exact friction.
If it feels aligned, I'd love to share details."

Energetic Reminder:
You're not selling.
You're offering stabilized clarity for those ready to receive it.

DAY 3 — The Content Seed

Create one piece of value-driven content related to your offer:

- A simple video breaking down one key misconception your client faces.

- A carousel post (if on Instagram) explaining 3 shifts they need to make.

- A short blog or email unpacking a common pricing block.

- A live video explaining your method and who it's for.

The content is not to "sell hard."
It's to **radiate clarity and authority** into the field.

Energetic Frame:

"I serve by transmitting clarity.
The right people will feel my field."

The Purpose of the 72-Hour Ritual

- Collapses overthinking.

- Stabilizes your offer energetically.

- Gives your nervous system reference points of being seen and safe.

- Activates the field of magnetic wealth creation.

**The Money Magnet Project is not about fast sales.
It's about stabilized field expansion.**

You will adjust, refine, and scale later.
But your field must move first.

Final Energetic Lock:

At the end of your 3rd day, speak:

"I have entered the field.
My wealth structure holds clarity.
My offer carries authority.
My visibility is clean.
I am ready to receive."

Protocol VII — The Visibility Protocol

Wealth is Attracted to Clarity, Boldness, and Precision

You are not paid for how talented you are.
You are paid for how clearly your value is perceived.

Most people struggling with wealth don't have a skill problem.
They have a **visibility problem.**

- They do great work in secret.

- They overthink how others will respond.

- They hesitate to show their authority.

- They shrink their message into vagueness.

Wealth does not respond to hidden energy.

Your offer can be powerful.
Your system can be clean.
But if your field is not visible, wealth cannot locate you.

The Visibility Distortion

Most people carry one or more visibility parasites:

- "I don't want to seem arrogant."

- "I'm still working on myself first."

- "I don't want to bother people."

- "What if they reject me?"

- "I'm not ready for that level yet."

These are not truths.
They are **field distortions.**

Visibility is not attention-seeking.
Visibility is transmission.

The Law of Visibility

Clarity attracts.
Boldness signals authority.
Precision eliminates confusion.

- When people feel your clarity, they trust you.

- When people feel your boldness, they lean in.

- When people feel your precision, they know exactly how to enter your field.

Visibility is how wealth scans for its next assignment.

Visibility Is Energetic Exposure

Being visible is not "posting more."
It is about transmitting:

- **Your offer** (clear outcome)

- **Your process** (how you move people)

- **Your standards** (who you serve and who you don't)

- **Your tone** (the energy you stabilize)

The clearer your signal, the cleaner your clients will self-select.

The Wealth Visibility Triangle

Your visibility sharpens across 3 energetic pillars:

---

1. Clarity: Your Message

- What problem do you solve?

- Who do you serve?

- What outcome do you create?

If they can't say it back to you after reading your post — you aren't clear enough.

---

2. Boldness: Your Presence

- Are you hiding behind disclaimers?

- Are you waiting for permission?

- Do you show up in full authority of your process?

Boldness doesn't mean force.
Boldness means **unapologetic presence.**

---

3. Precision: Your Call

- Do people know how to enter your offer?

- Is your invitation simple?

- Are your next steps visible?

If people are confused about what to do next, wealth stalls at the door.

The Energetic Frame Shift:

Visibility is not about convincing.
Visibility is about resonance.

You are not chasing.
You are **holding space** for those calibrated to your field.

Your Presence, Language, and Public Identity Influence Income

Your income rises to meet the stability of your field — and your field speaks through your presence.

Visibility isn't just about being seen.
It's about **how you are seen.**

- What energy you radiate.

- What words you use.

- What identity you embody publicly.

People don't buy your product first.
They buy your field.

---

1. Presence: The Energy That Enters First

Presence is the invisible force behind your visibility.
It's not appearance. It's not charisma.
It's your **calibrated signal of authority, safety, and clarity.**

When presence is clean:

- You feel relaxed while visible.

- You speak without overexplaining.

- You set boundaries without apology.

- Your body language carries certainty.

When presence is distorted:

- You compensate through over-teaching.

- You shrink your pricing or invitation.

- You soften your language to avoid triggering others.

- You hesitate, overthinking how you'll be perceived.

Presence stabilizes nervous systems — yours and theirs.

---

2. Language: The Precision of Transmission

Your income rises or falls on how clearly you articulate your value.

Clarity is not about complex words.
It's about speaking to the exact tension your audience feels.

Weak language repels income:

- "I help people live their best life."

- "I offer support on your journey."

- "I provide holistic services."

Strong language pulls wealth toward you:

- "I help freelancers double their pricing without fear of losing clients."

- "I help burned-out executives regain energy through daily nervous system recalibration."

- "I help spiritual practitioners build scalable online offers without losing integrity."

Clarity collapses hesitation.

When your language hits the exact pain your client feels, trust is instantly activated.

---

3. Public Identity: The Container They Buy Into

People don't buy your knowledge.
They buy your identity container.

Public identity is how you allow your expertise to exist in the world.

- Are you fully positioned as a guide for your specific solution?

- Does your content reflect your embodied process?

- Do your boundaries, pricing, and positioning match your energetic capacity?

- Are you building a consistent identity people can confidently enter?

When your public identity is clean:

- Your audience knows exactly what you do.

- They know how you help.

- They see your work as stable, trustworthy, and repeatable.

The Hidden Wealth Law Behind Visibility:

Confusion repels currency.
Coherence attracts contracts.

The more **stable your presence**, the more **clear your language**, the more **consistent your identity**, the faster income locates your field.

You don't have to "sell harder."
You have to **remove energetic fog.**

Challenge: Make Something Visible Within 72 Hours

Visibility is a frequency.
Delay weakens it.
Movement stabilizes it.

You've done the internal rewiring.
You've extracted your offer.
Now it must leave your mind and enter the world.

This challenge isn't about **perfection** — it's about **field activation.**

Why 72 Hours?

Because your nervous system obeys momentum.

If you delay visibility:

- Fear grows.

- Parasite programs re-engage.

- Identity regression occurs.

If you activate visibility:

- Authority stabilizes.

- Energetic neutrality increases.

- Magnetic signals amplify.

The 72-hour window collapses hesitation before the mind has time to sabotage.

The Visibility Activation Formula

You will make your offer visible in **3 moves across 3 days.**

DAY 1 — Public Signal Drop

Post publicly on your most natural platform:

- Social media (Instagram, LinkedIn, Facebook, YouTube, TikTok)

- Email list (if applicable)

- Personal network (text, group messages, community platforms)

Your post must include:

- **WHO:** Who you serve

- **WHAT:** What problem you resolve

- **HOW:** Your simple process

- **OFFER:** The invitation to engage

Example Post:
"I'm opening 3 spots for freelancers who feel trapped undercharging their services.
In 4 weeks, I help you break pricing fear, set clear boundaries, and confidently hold premium rates.
Weekly private sessions. Full pricing audit. No more second-guessing.
DM me if you want one of these spots."

Energetic Frame:

"I am safe being seen.
I am not seeking approval — I am offering stabilized clarity."

DAY 2 — Direct Invitations

Identify 3–5 people already near your field who:

- Have voiced interest in the past

- Match your ideal client profile

- Are energetically aligned to receive

Message them directly — **not as a cold pitch, but as a sovereign offer.**

Example Message:
"Hey [Name], I'm launching a new container specifically for freelancers who want to finally stabilize their pricing and income without burnout.
I thought of you because I know you've been navigating this exact challenge.
No pressure — if it's something you'd want details on, I'd be happy to share."

Energetic Frame:

"I serve. I offer. I detach from outcome. My field remains clean regardless of response."

DAY 3 — Educational Transmission

Create one simple piece of content that **transmits your authority:**

- A short video: break down 1 key mistake your audience makes.

- A simple post: list 3 shifts required to solve their problem.

- A live session: walk through your core framework in 10-15 minutes.

- A simple PDF or carousel: visually explain your process.

Example:
"3 pricing myths that keep freelancers broke — and how to break them."

Energetic Frame:

"I don't need to convince. I transmit clarity. The field organizes from here."

What This Challenge Installs:

- Rapid energetic exposure.

- Nervous system desensitization to visibility fear.

- Embodied authority through action.

- Field magnetism through stabilized movement.

Your visibility doesn't need to be perfect.
It needs to be present.

Final Command After 72 Hours:

Speak aloud:

"My field is visible.
My authority is stabilized.
My wealth structure is active.
I am fully available for aligned clients to enter."

PART III — Inner Code, Outer Power

You've cleared the parasites.
You've stabilized your frequency.
You've built your wealth architecture.
You've entered visibility.

Now we go deeper — into **the invisible code that governs whether you can hold and expand wealth permanently.**

Wealth doesn't collapse because of bad tactics.
It collapses because of unstable internal programming:

- Scarcity reflexes

- Emotional co-dependency

- Identity sabotage

- Approval addiction

- Shadow loops

Your income ceiling is not technical.
It is encoded inside your nervous system's ability to hold expansion.

Part III is where you build the *internal scaffolding* required to permanently sustain wealth.

- You will install the **Mental Framework of the Wealthy** — so pressure no longer distorts your decisions.

- You will reclaim full **Emotional Sovereignty** — breaking dependency loops that silently control your behavior.

- You will confront and integrate your **Shadow Scripts** — burning self-sabotage at the root, not the symptom level.

Power is not built externally.
It is installed through invisible self-command.

When this work is stabilized, your external income becomes unshakable — because your field no longer panics as it expands.

Now we enter the domain of:
Permanent Stability.
Permanent Authority.
Permanent Wealth.

Protocol VIII — The Mental Framework of the Wealthy

How the Rich Think Differently Under Pressure

Wealth is not sustained through information.
Wealth is sustained through internal command under pressure.

Everyone is calm when everything is working.
The difference between unstable income and permanent wealth is revealed during:

- Market shifts.

- Unexpected expenses.

- Business slowdowns.

- Personal challenges.

- Client rejections.

- High-stakes decisions.

Expansion always triggers pressure.
The question is not: "Will pressure come?"
The question is: "What happens inside you when it does?"

The Two Operating Systems

At the highest level, there are only two mental frameworks:

---

1. The Scarcity Reflex

- Reacts emotionally to money movement.

- Collapses under uncertainty.

- Shifts decisions based on fear of loss.

- Panics when income drops temporarily.

- Obsessively chases safety instead of building stability.

Scarcity reflex says:

"If something shifts, I'm unsafe. I need to act now to fix it."

This is why many people sabotage during growth:

They **can't hold the temporary destabilization required for wealth to expand.**

---

2. The Wealth Calibration Response

- Stays neutral during temporary contraction.

- Holds long-term clarity through short-term shifts.

- Sees data where others see danger.

- Protects boundaries even when tempted to over-deliver.

- Moves with strategy, not emotion.

Wealth calibration says:

"Fluctuations are normal. My field remains stable. I correct without collapse."

Why This Mental Code Is Non-Negotiable

The level of wealth you hold is the amount of pressure your nervous system can handle without panicking.

- As you scale income, pressure increases.

- As you expand visibility, exposure increases.

- As you raise prices, rejection risk increases.

You're not being tested.
You're being **trained to hold power without collapse.**

The Wealth Calibration Principle

The wealthy don't avoid pressure.
They practice remaining sovereign inside it.

- They don't price-drop in panic.

- They don't over-promise to "save" a client.

- They don't self-abandon for temporary comfort.

- They don't dismantle their systems at the first sign of contraction.

Their nervous system holds:

"I trust my structure.
I trust my field.
I trust my decisions."

The False Comfort of "Action"

Many people confuse urgency with productivity.

- They launch random sales when income dips.

- They add new offers to "fix" the problem.

- They seek new certifications to soothe insecurity.

- They hire coaches or mentors hoping for rescue.

This is not real growth — it's **emotional regulation disguised as business moves.**

The True Shift You Must Install:

Stabilize your nervous system before adjusting your actions.

- Breathe before reacting.

- Audit data before assumptions.

- Return to your protocols before inventing new ones.

- Trust containment before chasing more work.

Exercise: 15-Minute Daily Identity Conditioning Ritual

You've just seen how most people collapse under pressure because their nervous system isn't trained to hold expansion.
Now we're not just observing the pattern — we're breaking it.
This ritual installs the new default: calm authority inside pressure.
You're not hoping for stability — you're programming it.

You don't hold this identity by thinking.
You hold it by conditioning.

The difference between those who sustain wealth and those who constantly reset is this:

- The unstable try to *feel ready* before action.

- The wealthy *condition readiness* before the mind has time to distort.

This ritual installs your **Wealth Calibration Identity** into your nervous system daily — so when pressure hits, your field doesn't collapse.

The Structure: 15 Minutes Per Day

---

1. The Stabilization Anchor (2 Minutes)

Before you begin, regulate your body:

- Stand or sit tall.

- Shoulders back.

- Deep, slow breathing.

- Drop tension from face, jaw, and chest.

Speak softly:

"I am safe with expansion.
Pressure refines me.
My field is stable."

---

2. The Identity Embodiment Script (3 Minutes)

Speak these aloud — with full energetic command:

"I hold authority over my wealth field.
I do not chase — I calibrate.
Pressure reveals my stability.
I hold pricing without apology.
I hold visibility without collapse.
I hold decisions without panic.
My wealth expands because I contain power."

---

3. The Scenario Rehearsal (5 Minutes)

Mentally walk through **one scenario where pressure might arise:**

- A client questioning your price.

- A slow sales period.

- An unexpected large expense.

- Public rejection or critique.

Rehearse staying grounded:

- Feel the nervous system remain calm.

- Hold your breathing steady.

- See yourself responding with clarity, not collapse.

This trains your nervous system to associate pressure with stability — not survival.

---

4. The Calibration Audit (5 Minutes)

Journal quickly:

1. *Where did I remain stable under pressure yesterday?*
2. *Where did I feel pulled into scarcity reflexes?*
3. *What micro-shift will I install today?*

Why This Ritual Works

- Pressure triggers unconscious scripts.

- Rehearsal creates **pre-installed responses.**

- Daily repetition rewires identity at the nervous system level.

You're not "getting better."
You're installing authority.

Final Command After Each Session:

Speak softly to seal:

"I am conditioned for wealth stability.
My nervous system holds expansion.
My field remains sovereign."

Protocol IX — Emotional Sovereignty

Emotional Dependency Blocks Clarity and Wealth

Wealth requires authority — not just financially, but emotionally.

Most people unconsciously leak their power not because they lack skill, but because they are emotionally dependent on:

- Approval

- Validation

- Acceptance

- Praise

- Permission

- Belonging

Every one of these dependencies distorts your wealth field.

The Hidden Cost of Emotional Dependency

When your nervous system is wired to avoid disapproval, your financial decisions become contaminated.

You:

- Lower prices to avoid conflict.

- Overdeliver to be liked.

- Tolerate clients who drain you.

- Stay in low-value offers to stay "safe."

- Delay visibility to avoid judgment.

126

- Accept deals that feel heavy just to maintain comfort.

- Say "yes" when you know it should be "no."

The real cost isn't financial first — it's energetic.

- You lose clarity.

- You blur your standards.

- You betray your pricing.

- You resent your clients or audience silently.

Every act of emotional dependency fractures your authority field.

Why This Sabotages Wealth

Wealth flows through **decisive, sovereign containers** — not through emotional negotiation.

When you operate from dependency, your field sends this signal:

"I don't fully trust myself to hold this standard."

And wealth reads that instability as:

"The container is not ready to expand."

Emotional Sovereignty Is The Missing Piece

Sovereignty is not coldness.
Sovereignty is unhooking your identity from external reactions.

- You can love others without compromising your pricing.

- You can serve others without abandoning your boundaries.

- You can care for others without negotiating your authority.

The Emotional Sovereignty Principle:

Your wealth expands in direct proportion to your capacity to disappoint others without abandoning yourself.

This is where most can't hold:

- Fear of being disliked.

- Fear of being misunderstood.

- Fear of losing clients.

- Fear of family disapproval.

- Fear of looking "too confident."

So they shrink.
And shrinking kills income.

Why You Must Cut The Cords

- Because you cannot build stable wealth while your nervous system is still wired to seek external safety.

- Because you cannot price cleanly while negotiating self-worth.

- Because you cannot scale authority while fearing visibility judgment.

Emotional dependency is one of the last hidden parasites that survives even after tactical wealth-building begins.

How to Reclaim Power, Say No, and Unhook Your Identity from Approval

Sovereignty isn't built by controlling others.
Sovereignty is built by commanding yourself when pressure rises.

You don't lose wealth because of bad clients, toxic family, or difficult conversations.
You lose wealth when you abandon your standards to keep others comfortable.

Every time you avoid saying "no" to protect harmony, you sign an invisible contract:

"I agree to shrink my power so you stay comfortable."

Wealth does not tolerate that contract.
Wealth requires clean boundaries.

Why Most People Struggle to Say No

Beneath every people-pleasing reflex lives:

- The fear of abandonment.

- The fear of being "too much."

- The fear of being rejected.

- The fear of losing love or connection.

- The fear of disappointing those they serve.

These fears don't come from logic — they're survival reflexes embedded long before wealth was ever a question.

This is why even powerful, skilled people:

- Undersell themselves.

- Overdeliver.

- Lower prices for certain people.

- Say yes when every part of them wants to say no.

Why "Approval Addiction" Is the Hidden Saboteur

As long as your nervous system requires others to feel safe, you will subconsciously cap your wealth.

- You won't fully market your offer.

- You'll avoid polarizing your message.

- You'll hesitate to charge authority-level pricing.

- You'll tolerate draining relationships.

- You'll shrink your presence when others feel threatened.

The Shift: Authority Over Approval

Saying "no" isn't aggression.
It's alignment.

Sovereignty is not coldness — it's stability.

When you stop negotiating your standards, your nervous system stabilizes.
And when your nervous system stabilizes, your wealth expands.

The 3 Energetic Frames to Install

---

1. Detach Identity From Response

"Their discomfort is not my identity."

When others feel tension from your boundaries, you must separate:

- **Their emotional response** (their responsibility)

- **Your decision** (your sovereignty)

You are not responsible for managing their nervous system.

---

2. Hold Standards Without Explanation

"I do not explain my boundaries."

When you start justifying your "no," you invite debate.

- State your boundary once.

- State it clearly.

- Hold it without nervous energy.

Sovereignty speaks once.

---

3. Align Discomfort with Expansion

"Every time I hold my standard, I stretch my capacity to contain more wealth."

You will feel temporary discomfort when breaking old approval contracts.

That discomfort is not a warning.
It's **growth pain**.

The Wealth Law Behind Sovereignty:

The wealth you desire already exists.
It simply requires a container strong enough to hold it.

Sovereignty is the steel frame that holds expanding wealth.

Tools: Cord-Cutting Script + 24-Hour Sovereignty Reset

You are not losing people.
You are losing the invisible chains that have controlled your field.

Emotional cords are not always conscious.
They're energetic contracts you've silently agreed to over years:

- "I'll stay small so you're comfortable."

- "I'll tolerate this client so I feel needed."

- "I'll keep these prices low so no one gets upset."

- "I'll hide my ambition so I'm not abandoned."

The longer these cords remain, the more distorted your wealth field becomes.

We are not cutting love.
We are cutting energetic dependency.

The Cord-Cutting Script

This is not a one-time ritual.
This is a **field maintenance tool** — used whenever you feel entangled with someone else's emotions or approval.

The Process:

- Sit still. Close your eyes.

- Breathe deeply until your chest softens.

- Visualize the person, client, or entity where tension exists.

- See a cord connecting you — from your solar plexus (power center) to theirs.

Speak slowly, powerfully:

"I honor the role you've played.
I release you from responsibility for my safety.
I revoke the contract that tied my worth to your response.
I hold my field sovereign and complete.
You are free. I am free."

- Visualize the cord dissolving in light.

- Feel your energy returning fully to your body.

- Sit for one minute in stillness after.

This is not aggression.
This is field clarity.

You do not owe anyone the sacrifice of your wealth stability.

The 24-Hour Sovereignty Reset

Sometimes, after cord cutting, subtle emotional residue lingers — like phantom programs running silently.

This reset clears those echoes before they regain control.

For 24 Hours:

1. Speak NO explanations when you decline something.
2. Avoid scanning others for approval after decisions.
3. Pause before replying to any request — breathe, feel, then respond.
4. Repeat this command every time anxiety arises:

"I do not need permission to hold my authority.
My wealth field is stabilized by clarity — not by approval."

5. Write this on paper and carry it with you:

*"My safety is not negotiated externally.
My wealth expands as I stabilize my identity internally."*

The Law of Emotional Containment

Every time you reclaim power from emotional dependency, you widen the bandwidth your field can hold.

Your nervous system stops associating "being liked" with "being safe."

And when that loop is broken — wealth begins flowing through authority, not negotiation.

Protocol X — Shadow Integration

Self-Sabotage Isn't Random — It's Scripted

You are not broken.
You are running programs.

Most people blame themselves for "sabotage":

- Procrastinating right before expansion.

- Undercharging after breakthroughs.

- Avoiding visibility when growth arrives.

- Starting offers — then freezing.

- Building income — then draining it.

They call this self-sabotage.
But in reality, these are not random acts.
These are old **identity scripts** playing out for one purpose:
Protection.

Why Self-Sabotage Is a Survival Reflex

Your shadow doesn't hate your success.
Your shadow fears the consequences of change.

Every identity you've held is built on:

- Safety patterns.

- Emotional contracts.

- Nervous system regulation loops.

- Family, cultural, and personal survival strategies.

When you grow, you threaten those structures.

The shadow rises not to destroy you — but to keep you inside the familiar.

The Script Behind the Sabotage

Every time you sabotage wealth, visibility, or expansion, you are unconsciously protecting yourself from:

- Abandonment

- Rejection

- Exposure

- Responsibility

- Being "too powerful" for your circle

- Outgrowing your tribe or identity group

The sabotage is not irrational — it's rehearsed protection.

The Shadow Program Examples

Let's call them out directly:

- **"If I grow too fast, I'll lose control."**

- **"If I charge more, I'll lose love or connection."**

- **"If I become visible, I'll attract criticism or envy."**

- **"If I leave this job, I'll disappoint my family."**

- **"If I succeed too much, something bad will happen to balance it."**

- **"If I fully embody authority, I won't be relatable anymore."**

These are not random thoughts.
These are defense mechanisms deeply programmed into your nervous system.

Why Shadow Integration Is Required for Wealth

You cannot bypass the shadow.
You must integrate it.

- The shadow is not the enemy.

- It holds your unclaimed power.

- But you must extract the power while neutralizing the distortion.

Wealth will not stabilize while your shadow scripts secretly run protection programs every time expansion arrives.

The Hidden Wealth Law Behind Shadow Work:

The version of you that holds wealth effortlessly is the version that no longer fears who they become when expansion arrives.

Your wealth ceiling is simply the emotional bandwidth you have for:

- Power

- Visibility

- Responsibility

- Freedom

The shadow keeps that bandwidth artificially low — until you burn the script.

Learn to Spot Your Patterns, Then Burn the Script

You cannot burn what you refuse to see.
The first wealth skill is detection.

Most self-sabotage happens because people don't recognize *how predictable* their patterns really are.

They believe:

- "I just have a motivation problem."

- "I get in my head sometimes."

- "I need more discipline."

- "I should work harder."

Wrong.

You don't have random discipline problems.
You have deeply rehearsed identity protection patterns.

The Sabotage Cycle (How the Script Plays Out)

1. Trigger Appears:
An opportunity for growth appears (pricing increase, client expansion, visibility).

2. Nervous System Activates:
Subconscious fear gets triggered (loss of control, rejection, judgment).

3. Protective Logic Engages:
The mind creates rationalizations:

- "It's not the right time."

- "I don't feel fully ready."

- "I should wait until I'm more qualified."

- "I'll work on it next month."

4. Behavioral Freeze or Collapse:

- Delay.

- Procrastination.

- Over-preparing.

- Self-imposed chaos.

- Income plateau.

5. Relief Arrives:
Temporary safety returns — no expansion, no threat.

The script succeeds. You stay safe, small, contained.

The Emotional Pattern Behind It

Every sabotage loop is rooted in safety — not laziness.

You aren't avoiding success.
You're avoiding:

- Feeling unsafe with more money.

- The pressure of higher visibility.

- The fear of being resented by family or peers.

- The guilt of surpassing others.

- The terror of being fully responsible for bigger outcomes.

The shadow whispers:
"If I stay here, I'll stay safe."

The Key to Burning the Script: Pattern Recognition

You must become ruthless in spotting:

- **When you delay after success.**

- **When you discount your pricing before presenting.**

- **When you avoid visibility right after receiving attention.**

- **When you seek "one more training" instead of launching.**

- **When you default to safety-mode in your business, relationships, or offers.**

The moment you see the script, it begins losing power.

The Personal Shadow Audit (Self-Diagnosis Tool)

Write these out now:

1. *Where do I consistently self-limit when opportunity appears?*
2. *What is the story I always tell myself in those moments?*
3. *What am I protecting myself from emotionally?*
4. *Whose voice does this pattern resemble? (parent, culture, past identity, etc.)*
5. *What have I already lost or delayed because of this pattern?*

Do not self-edit.
This is confrontation work — not self-soothing work.

The Shadow Law:

Your wealth expansion begins when you stop confusing protection with progress.

You are not fragile.
You are not fragile.
You are not fragile.

The shadow simply convinced you that you were.

141

Ritual: The Shadow Confrontation + Self-Replacement Exercise

You cannot negotiate with the shadow.
You confront it. You extract its power. You rewrite the command.

Step 1 — Name The Script

Sit in stillness. Breathe deeply. Allow the core pattern to rise.

Write this out fully:

1. *What is the recurring sabotage loop I keep running?*
2. *What does my mind always say in those moments?*
3. *What emotion rises when expansion shows up?*
4. *What am I really protecting myself from?*

Example:

- "I delay launching every time I'm about to go public."

- "I always say, 'I just need to refine it more.'"

- "The emotion is fear of public judgment."

- "I'm protecting myself from visibility rejection."

The more specific, the more powerful.

Step 2 — Speak the Confrontation

Speak these words out loud, slowly, with authority:

"I see you.
You are not my weakness.
You were installed to protect me from pain.
But I no longer need this protection.
This script is not my identity.

142

I revoke the contract.
I release the fear.
I hold the authority."

Pause. Let the nervous system feel the words fully.

Step 3 — The Self-Replacement Declaration

Now write the *opposite command* — the identity you are stabilizing:

"I am fully capable of holding expansion.
I stand visible in my power.
I carry wealth without fear.
I am safe in authority.
I welcome responsibility with clarity.
My nervous system holds increasing wealth with stability."

Step 4 — Embody the Identity Loop (3-Minute Drill)

Stand up.

- Shoulders open.

- Chest tall.

- Breathe deeply.

- Speak your Self-Replacement Declaration aloud 3 times, each time stronger.

Feel the words enter your nervous system as *default programming* — not wishful thinking.

Step 5 — Anchor the New Program

For the next 7 days:

- Speak your Self-Replacement Declaration each morning upon waking.

- Speak it anytime resistance rises.

- Write it once daily by hand.

Repetition re-codes the field.

This isn't affirmation.

This is nervous system rewiring.

The Shadow Law:

**The old script will attempt to reassert itself.
But repetition collapses its authority.**

You don't need to negotiate anymore.
You've replaced the operator of your system.

PART IV — Embodiment & Exit

You've purged the parasites.
You've recoded your frequency.
You've stabilized your wealth structure.
You've burned the sabotage scripts.

Now we move into **embodiment and final exit.**
Many people build internal power — but stop short of full expression.
They still **act like the old version of themselves**, even after doing the work.

- They dress like who they were.

- They speak like who they were.

- They move like who they were.

- They live inside structures designed for survival, not sovereignty.

Embodiment is when your identity becomes non-negotiable.
Exit is when your external life reflects that internal authority.
This final part installs:

- The daily embodiment of wealth authority.

- The behavioral alignment that stabilizes your magnetism.

- The design of your financial exit plan — to remove yourself from systems that keep most people enslaved to burnout, dependency, and energetic debt.

Wealth isn't fully stabilized until your nervous system, behavior, and external systems all mirror the same authority.

Here, you will no longer "try to hold" wealth.

You will become wealth.

145

Protocol XI — The Wealth Embodiment Shift

You Become What You Consistently Carry

Wealth is not an outcome.
Wealth is a state you stabilize.

At this stage, the work is no longer about:

- Clearing more blocks

- Running new rituals

- Consuming more information

Now it's about **daily embodiment**.
Because your nervous system has been trained, your structure has been built, and your field has been cleaned.

But unless you carry wealth energetically, behaviorally, and visually — the field will remain at partial capacity.

The Myth That Keeps People Stuck

Most people still unconsciously believe:

- *"When I make more, I'll finally feel wealthy."*

- *"When I hit that goal, I'll upgrade how I move."*

This is backwards.

You don't act wealthy because you have money.
You stabilize wealth, and the money follows.

You become wealth first — through:

- Posture

- Language

- Environment

- Movement

- Decisions

- Boundaries

Your nervous system reads these daily signals as:
"We are safe with expansion."

The Identity Frequency You Now Install

You are training your entire field to hold wealth as normal.

Wealth embodiment means:

- How you answer messages.

- How you decline offers.

- How you respond to delays.

- How you hold pricing.

- How you walk into rooms.

- How you dress, speak, and present yourself publicly and privately.

These micro-signals are not "style."
They are field signals.

Your field cannot hold wealth you're afraid to embody.

The Magnetic Reality of Embodiment

People don't buy your service first — they buy your stability.

When you:

- Speak with simplicity, not justification.

- Move without urgency or rush.

- Set pricing and hold it.

- Dress like someone who respects their body and field.

- Walk with an inner calm that does not seek external approval.

Wealth finds you faster.
Opportunities locate you naturally.
Boundaries protect themselves.

Because your field now signals:
"I am safe to receive and contain more."

Why Most People Resist This Phase

- They fear seeming arrogant.

- They fear others will criticize their confidence.

- They fear outgrowing their current circle.

- They wait for permission.

But **embodiment isn't arrogance.**

Embodiment is alignment.

You are simply matching your internal power with external congruence.

The Embodiment Law:

Your external world organizes itself according to your embodied frequency.

When your behavior, environment, language, and posture match your wealth identity, you no longer have to "work on wealth."
You are wealth.

Dress, Move, Speak, and Show Up Like Someone Wealth Flows To

You don't attract wealth through effort.
You attract it through frequency consistency.

Your field communicates before you ever open your mouth.

- How you move.

- How you present.

- How you enter rooms.

- How you dress.

- How you speak.

- How you make decisions.

Every action either reinforces your wealth field or destabilizes it.

---

1. Dress: Wear the Identity You're Stabilizing

Clothing is energetic programming.

You don't need designer labels or luxury brands.
You need congruence.

- Wear what signals self-respect.

- Eliminate clothing that represents old versions of yourself (cheap, careless, or shrinking choices).

- Choose pieces that feel clean, elevated, and intentional — even if simple.

You are broadcasting to your nervous system:
"We take ourselves seriously."

Wealth resists fields that dress for survival.
It gravitates toward fields that signal stability.

---

2. Move: Occupy Space Like You Belong

Wealth flows to those who normalize expansion.

How you physically carry yourself matters:

- Shoulders back.

- Chest open.

- Chin slightly elevated.

- Eyes present.

- Movements intentional, not rushed or jittery.

Your movement teaches your nervous system:

"I am safe holding more space."

Rushed, collapsed posture signals the opposite:

- *"I don't belong here."*

- *"I hope I'm accepted."*

You are not asking for permission to expand.
You are stabilizing the expansion as normal.

---

3. Speak: Language as a Wealth Signal

Words stabilize or fragment the wealth field.

Every word you speak either:

- Reinforces authority

151

- Signals insecurity

Low-frequency language:

- "I'm just getting started."

- "Hopefully this works."

- "I know it's a lot of money…"

- "If that's okay with you…"

Wealth-stabilizing language:

- "Here's the investment."

- "This is the process I deliver."

- "I serve [who] to achieve [outcome]."

- "This is my capacity for this round."

Precision = stability.

---

4. Show Up: Normalize Visibility

Wealth cannot find you if you stay hidden.

Showing up means:

- Being publicly visible inside your authority.

- Posting consistently.

- Sharing your frameworks.

- Holding polarizing clarity when necessary.

- Being seen fully in your energetic tone.

You cannot receive at scale while remaining energetically invisible.

152

The more you stabilize your visibility, the more wealth recognizes your field as **structurally prepared** to hold expansion.

The Embodiment Law Expanded:

Wealth mirrors stability, not performance.

You are not performing wealth.
You are normalizing it through:

- Repetition

- Alignment

- Energetic consistency

When your dress, movement, language, and visibility all carry the same frequency, wealth enters without resistance.

Protocol XII — Exit the Trap (Spiritually + Structurally)

Remove Yourself From Systems That Drain You — Physically and Mentally

You were not born into wealth slavery.
You were trained into it.

The external world is built to keep most people:

- Energetically depleted.

- Financially dependent.

- Over-leveraged into debt cycles.

- Emotionally entangled with survival traps.

- Subtly obedient to systems designed to extract, not empower.

You do not escape by fighting the system.
You exit by building your own field of sovereignty.

The Hidden Systems That Quietly Drain Most People

Let's name them directly:

- Employment structures that exchange time for capped wages.

- Consumer debt systems designed to keep you emotionally regulated through spending.

- Health systems that manage symptoms but preserve dependency.

- Family and cultural programming that teach guilt-based obligation.

154

- Education models that train obedience, not critical sovereignty.

- Marketing systems that prey on insecurity to create endless "solutions."

**Most people stay trapped not because they don't work —
but because they work inside structures designed to absorb their labor and leave them exhausted.**

The Two Types of Traps

1. The Spiritual Trap:

- Internalized guilt, obligation, fear of outgrowing others.

- Emotional entanglements that make sovereignty feel selfish.

- Fear of being abandoned if you fully rise.

2. The Structural Trap:

- Financial dependency on unstable income streams.

- No exit plan from trading hours for money.

- No scalable offers or wealth systems installed.

- Debt structures that replicate survival even at higher income levels.

**The spiritual trap keeps you emotionally small.
The structural trap keeps you financially tied.**

Both must be exited.

Why Most People Stay Stuck

Because comfort feels safer than freedom.

The system rewards you with:

- Social approval.

- Predictable discomfort.

- False security.

- Steady dissatisfaction.

- Controlled expansion ceilings.

Freedom feels scarier at first — because it requires personal authority.

The Exit Law:

You cannot build sovereign wealth inside systems designed for dependency.

The moment you choose sovereignty:

- You will lose some approval.

- You will confront temporary instability.

- You will restructure how you work, move, and relate.

But you will reclaim authority over your time, energy, and expansion permanently.

Build Your Stealth Plan for Freedom, Flow, and Peace

You don't announce your exit.
You construct it quietly, precisely, and without permission.

The system expects people to stay trapped.
It expects:

- Endless hustle.

- Repeating debt cycles.

- Sacrificing health for income.

- Trading sovereignty for "security."

But when you exit correctly, you leave behind both the burnout and the dependence — permanently.

The 3 Pillars of the Stealth Exit Plan

---

1. Energy Exit: Cleanse the Emotional Cords

- Audit every person, group, or institution where obligation still overrides sovereignty.

- Release emotional contracts disguised as loyalty.

- Create emotional distance from people whose energy pulls you back into old frequencies.

Freedom requires emotional clarity before financial freedom can stabilize.

---

2. Financial Exit: Design Your Personal Wealth Engine

You no longer chase "more income." You design:

- **Scalable income streams:**
  Clean offers, recurring revenue, digital products, client containers.

- **Containment structures:**
  Simplified business models, no constant customization, clear boundaries.

- **The Money Flow Grid:**
  Automated financial organization that holds rising wealth without chaos.

- **Debt purge strategy:**
  Aggressive but controlled elimination of any debt structures.

You stop building income for survival.
You build it for sovereignty and time control.

---

3. System Exit: Architect Your Structural Independence

- Build work models that are location-flexible.

- Eliminate dependencies on single clients, companies, or platforms.

- Digitize knowledge where possible to create leveraged income.

- Build operating systems (personal and business) that run whether you're "on" or not.

You don't escape systems.
You build your own system that serves you.

The Core Design Question:

"If everything stopped tomorrow — would my income, nervous system, and lifestyle remain intact for 90 days?"

If not:

- The stealth plan begins now.

- Quietly, systematically, relentlessly.

The Stealth Exit Timeline

Phase	Focus
Phase 1: Containment	Stabilize spending, seal energetic leaks, clean financial structure.
Phase 2: Sovereign Offers	Build scalable offers that reflect your clean authority.
Phase 3: Visibility Control	Expand visibility in alignment with your nervous system's capacity.
Phase 4: Financial Buffer	Build cash reserves, debt neutralization, emergency fund.
Phase 5: Exit Activation	Gradual release from dependency structures (employment, toxic clients, unnecessary obligations).

The system was built for your exhaustion.
You are building a system for your peace.

The Exit Command:

Speak aloud:

"I release dependency.
I release guilt.
I release systems that no longer serve my expansion.
I install sovereignty.
I stabilize wealth by design, not by permission."

Final Ritual: Write Your Protocol Command & Build Your Plan

You don't need another course.
You don't need more strategy.
You don't need to "get ready."
You are now installed.

You've purged parasites.
You've recoded frequency.
You've stabilized wealth systems.
You've burned the sabotage scripts.
You've embodied authority.
You've exited the traps.

Now you leave this work **as a new operator of your wealth field.**

This ritual seals the entire protocol into your nervous system — not as an idea, but as your new normal.

Step 1 — Write Your Protocol Command

Take a blank page.
Write your **personalized wealth command.**

Use this structure as your guide:

"I command my field to operate at sovereign wealth frequency.
I no longer submit to [insert key patterns you've burned].
My income stabilizes through [insert your value loops & scalable offers].
My emotional field remains clear of [insert emotional dependencies].
My nervous system holds expansion with authority.
I am safe, powerful, and fully stabilized inside wealth.
My exit is complete. My expansion is permanent."

Write until you feel a full-body energetic release.

Step 2 — Build Your Activation Plan

This plan is not another "goal list."
It is your **sovereign execution map**.

Divide your next 90 days into 3 clear categories:

---

1. Energetic Stability

- Daily identity conditioning (Protocol VIII)

- Embodiment journaling (Protocol XI)

- Shadow recalibrations (Protocol X)

---

2. Financial Infrastructure

- Finalize scalable offers (Protocol VI)

- Continue sealing financial leaks (Protocol V)

- Expand visibility cycles (Protocol VII)

- Complete stealth exit milestones (Protocol XII)

---

3. Field Integrity

- Weekly sovereignty audits:

    o   Where am I still seeking approval?

    o   Where am I still negotiating boundaries?

    o   Where am I leaking power in relationships, decisions, or pricing?

You are now maintaining your authority — not searching for it.

The Closing Command

Speak this aloud:

"I walk forward as the stabilized version of myself.
My wealth is not coming — it is present.
My expansion is not future — it is active.
I hold authority without collapse.
I embody sovereignty without negotiation.
I am the operator of my wealth field.
It is done."

Final Words: A Thank You

You didn't just read a book.
You entered a system.
A system designed not to motivate you, but to **recalibrate you**.

You faced patterns most people never name.
You purged parasites that had lived quietly for years.
You rewired your nervous system to hold power instead of collapse.
You stopped negotiating your wealth.
You stopped chasing freedom and instead **installed sovereignty**.

This was not light work.
This was not entertainment.
This was confrontation, extraction, and command.

And you chose to walk it.

The wealth you carry forward now isn't just income.
It's authority.
It's clarity.
It's peace.

You have exited the cycle that traps millions.
You have reclaimed your field.

As you move forward, remember:

Wealth isn't something you pursue.
Wealth is something you stabilize.

Thank you for having the courage to step into this work.
The system was never built for you to win.
But you just exited the system.

I honor the version of you that now walks in permanent sovereignty.

It is done.

www.ingramcontent.com/pod-product-compliance
Lightning Source LLC
Chambersburg PA
CBHW070403200326
41518CB00011B/2045